Make a Movie
That Tells A Story
· ·
Using a Home Camcorder...
...and Other Stuff You Already Own

by

Billy Field

MAKE A MOVIE.NET™
A Worldwide Network of Students Making Movies™
www.makeamovie.net

Published by William Field
Post Office Drawer 1549
Tuscaloosa, Alabama 35403

www.makeamovie.net

Phone: (205) 345-0443

Make A Movie.Net, *A Worldwide Network of Students Making Movies*™
and The Hero Next Door™
are trademarks of William Field.

Printed in the United States of America

Design by Susan J. Scruggs & David E. Craig

Education Edition
ISBN 0-9667470-1-1

ACKNOWLEDGMENTS

I want to thank my writer friends Charlie Cobean, John Binder and Wayne Greenhaw for their thoughts on the book. I want to thank Robin Cooper-Stone, Andy Stone and Jennifer Horne for their fresh eyes and insight during the editing process. Thanks to two of my former "star" students for reading the manuscript, Sam Stumpf and Jeff Weaver, both of whom have, by now, written, directed and edited their own feature films. I want to thank Rickey Yanaura for the photographs, Susan Scruggs and David Craig for designing the book. Special thanks to my friend G.W. Bailey for hosting the video. Finally, I want to thank all those who believed in this project and encouraged me to make it a reality.

*For L.B.F., teacher,
mother, grandmother.
And for J.W.F. who is,
as always, "the greatest."*

TABLE OF CONTENTS

1. Introduction 1

2. Story & Screenplay 5

3. Preproduction 27

4. Directing 37

5. Camera 55

6. Lighting 67

7. Sound 75

8. Editing 89

9. Digital Editing 103

10. Quik Flicks 113

11. The Hero Next Door™ 119

12. Support, Distribution, & the Future 137

INTRODUCTION

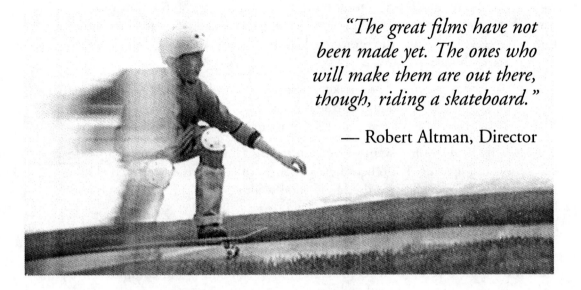

"The great films have not been made yet. The ones who will make them are out there, though, riding a skateboard."

— Robert Altman, Director

Talent exists. But talent does not guarantee success. Talent must be ignited—and nurtured. The kids Robert Altman is referring to may be in your classroom. I guarantee you this—some of those kids are in somebody's classroom. Part of the mission of this program is to ignite talent—and to provide you with enough information to nurture that talent, when you find it.

Another purpose of this program is to have fun. I've taught this program in schools, scouts and church and synagogue youth groups. It has been my experience that, while every kid doesn't necessarily want to be the next Steven Spielberg, most do, at least, have a lot of fun—acting, doing make-up, or shooting camera. At the very least this is a fun group activity. At the very best, it's a project that can discover talent, nurture talent and maybe even change the course of a student's life.

The basis of a story is a problem. The main character overcoming obstacles to solve that problem is the story. One of the places students learn to look for stories is in the problems they wrestle with in their everyday lives—like peer pressure. These problems will prove to be fertile ground for developing stories. If story conferences get students talking about their problems, even in the context of fiction, then those story conferences have value in ways other than making the movie.

When I was a kid, I wanted to make movies. We had an 8mm camera but no equipment for sound or editing. I made splices with scotch tape. I used a straightened paper clip to punch perforation holes through the tape, so the film would run through the projector. It wasn't a miracle if the movie told a story. It was a miracle if the splices went through the projector. I wanted to make movies, but there was nobody to teach me how.

Later, in college, my desire to make movies re-emerged. This time, there was somebody to guide me through the rough spots. I fell in love with making movies. I knew what I wanted to do with the rest of my life.

Following graduation, I went to work in the film business, doing editing, camera, sound and lighting. I also became a writer on three television series, including *FAME*. I wrote screenplays for the Hollywood studios. I've always felt proud and lucky to be part of the film business.

I created this training program for two reasons. First, I remembered when I was a kid and wanted to make movies, there was nobody to teach me how. My second reason had to do with recent breakthroughs in video and computer technology. Now, because of those breakthroughs, any student can make a movie that tells a story, complete with dialogue, sound effects, music and titles for, literally, the cost of the videotape. To me, someone who has always been obsessed with making movies, that's a miracle!

If one of your students starts this program when she is, say, fifteen, by the time she graduates from high school, that student could, for the price of ten fairly large lunches, make ten movies, each time learning what works and what doesn't work. By graduation, that student's knowledge of movie making could be light years ahead of where it was when she started. This program gives your students the opportunity to gain real experience, and that experience is pure gold—because experience is the true teacher.

When Steven Spielberg was on *The Larry King Show*, a mother called in and asked Spielberg what her son should do to learn how to make movies. Spielberg knew the answer right away. He told the caller that her son should get a camcorder and go out and make a movie. That's the best way to learn.

The book *Rebel Without A Crew* is the true story, told through a diary, of a young man, Robert Rodriguez, who made movies, using the same techniques we teach in this program. By the time Rodriguez graduated from high school, he'd made twelve movies, using his father's home video camera and editing on a home VCR. At the University of Texas, Rodriguez was the best student in his film making class because he'd actually had the experience of making movies. It didn't matter that he'd made those movies on a home camcorder and a VCR. The production and story telling techniques were the same.

Soon after college, Rodriguez sold his first feature length movie to a major Hollywood studio. He has gone on since to make more feature films. Desire, plus the experience of making those twelve movies are what gave Robert Rodriguez the chance to tell his stories to the world. You may not agree with his first movie (it's a little on the violent side), but that's not the point. The point is Robert Rodriguez learned to make movies doing the same things we teach in this program. What we teach here works!

This book is designed to lead you through simple, step-by-step lessons. I have also designed a video to supplement the book, teaching lessons that might be made more clear in motion pictures rather than text. The video does not, however, take the place of the book. It's important that you read the book before studying the video.

If you don't want to read through the entire book before starting your first movie, you have the option to go straight to "Quik Flicks." Quik Flicks is designed to get you started right away. Open the book. Read the Introduction and the chapter on "Story & Screenplay," then jump to Quik Flicks. Quik Flicks tells you the exact equipment you will need, how to come up with a quick story, and how to shoot it so that there's no editing equipment required.

The book also includes a chapter on our documentary program, *The Hero Next Door*™. *The Hero Next Door* provides the opportunity for students to discover a person who made a difference to the quality of life in their community—and to tell that person's story to the world. Many young people think their lives don't make a difference. Making this documentary is an opportunity for students to realize how any act of courage or kindness, no matter how small, can make a difference. We may not see it in our lifetime, but there is always a ripple effect. A recent Hollywood movie has a line where a mother says to her teenage son, "As long as you're alive on this earth, you have a choice." Students need to know that and the *Hero Next Door* is a way to remind them that it is true.

Make A Movie.Net offers training, support, and a place to go with your movie when it's finished. Trade it with other schools from across the country through the Trading Post, found on our web site at www.makeamovie.net. This "Cyber Studio" offers the opportunity for students from around the world to come together on the web to share their production ideas, their stories, and their excitement.

The promise of this book, video and training program is to teach you and your students how to make a movie that tells a story, using a home camcorder and other equipment you already own, or can borrow. This program is meant to be democratic, available to all kids, regardless of their financial situation. If you don't have money, you're lucky. Having no money forces you to solve the problem creatively, and that always gives you a better result than money would have in the first place, plus you learned something.

There's a saying in the South, "Talk don't pick no cotton." So let's stop talking and get into action. My promise to you is that I will keep these lessons simple. Your promise to me is that you will bring desire to this process and you won't give up. If you have the desire to make a movie that tells a story, then let's get started.

Story & Screenplay

When I first wanted to learn to write, I was told it was impossible to teach someone to write. That's not exactly the thing you want to hear, when that's exactly the thing you want to learn. I have since discovered that there are rules to help you build a story, the same way there are rules to help you build a house. After writing several stories, and embodying those rules, you are free to forget them. But, for now, you are learning. Anyone learning to play the guitar, without learning the chords, would be taking the long way around. Likewise, if you grab a note pad and feverishly begin to write a screenplay, you will soon be lost, wandering in the wilderness. Follow these lessons. They will lead you through the wilderness.

The first important lesson I want you to know is this: You know more than you think you know.

Deep inside, you understand movie stories because you've seen so many of them. When I describe the end of act one, you'll probably know what I'm talking about. You may not have known what to call it, but you'll recognize that beat, or that movement, in a movie story. The same will probably be true for the end of act two, for the climactic scene and for story elements like main character, problem, decision, goal and obstacles.

If we're going to make a movie, we need to write a screenplay. But we're not ready yet. The first thing we need is a story.

WHERE DO STORIES COME FROM?

The honest answer is "everywhere." Whenever you have a human being (or any other creature capable of making a decision) with a problem, you have the potential for a story.

A story is about a character who encounters a problem and struggles against obstacles to overcome that problem.

You can start with a character and add the problem. Or you can start with the problem and add the character. Either way, you'll find the spark, the basis, of a story if you add a third element—the decision.

A story is about a main character who encounters a problem and makes a decision to solve that problem. Potential stories are around us all the time because everywhere we look, there are people with problems. The thing that makes a story, though, is when a person makes a decision to overcome that problem. There are thousands of washed-up prize fighters. That's a problem. But it's not a story. It becomes a story, though, when one of them named Rocky makes a decision to fight the world champion.

The basis of a story is the main character struggling against obstacles to overcome a problem. In the movie *Lorenzo's Oil*, the father struggles against the disease that is killing his son by searching tirelessly for a cure. The father has a problem: His son is sick. The "or-else" factor is that someone must find a cure for his son's disease or else his son will die. The father makes a decision: To find a cure for his son's illness. The story is about the father's struggle to find that cure.

The audience wants to get caught up, emotionally, in the main character's struggle. They pay money to feel a part of that struggle. A turn-of-the-century theater critic, William Archer, said, "The audience goes to the theater to worry."

When a main character makes a decision, at that precise moment, the main character's goal is created. In *Lorenzo's Oil*, the goal is born at the moment the father makes the decision to find a cure for his son's illness. The goal is the thing that must be achieved in order to solve the problem. Rocky Balboa feels that he is a loser. That's his problem. His decision is to go fifteen rounds with the world champion to prove to himself that he's not a loser. Going fifteen rounds becomes his goal. He sets out to achieve it, no matter what!

In *ET, The Extraterrestrial*, Elliot is friends with ET. When ET needs to get home, that's a problem. Elliot's goal becomes to get ET safely home.

I started by saying there are basic elements for building a story. We've talked about three—character, problem and goal. Let's clarify those three and add a few more.

MAIN CHARACTER

There can be many characters in a movie story. Some may occupy as much screen-time as the main character, but there is only one main character. There are three criteria that separate the main character from other important characters in the story. First, the main character is the one who makes the decision to overcome the problem. Second, the main character must be active, not passive. The main character drives the action forward through his unrelenting pursuit of the goal. Third, the main character is the one who learns a lesson, or grows emotionally. In the early scenes of *ET*, Elliot is unsure of himself. By the end of the story, Elliot has grown emotionally. Through his struggle to get ET home, Elliot has discovered an inner strength he did not know he had.

PIVOTAL PROBLEM

There are all kinds of problems in a story. Problems are the gasoline that makes a story run. But there is only one pivotal problem. The story "pivots" on this problem. The little space creature, ET, is going to be caught and possibly used in a government experiment. That's a problem. When Elliot makes a decision to overcome that problem, everything in the story becomes about solving that problem. Sure, there are off-shoots here and there. But the spine of the story is about Elliot's efforts to solve that pivotal, or central, problem.

DECISION

There are people and problems everywhere. But if there is no decision to overcome the problem, there is no story.

You have the power to put a problem and a character together and make it a story, though, because you have the power to create a character who will make the decision to overcome the problem. That power is what makes you a writer.

GOAL

Reaching the goal will bring about the resolution of the problem. In *Lorenzo's Oil*, the father is the main character. The son's illness is the problem. The father makes a decision to overcome the problem by finding a cure. Finding the cure instantly becomes the goal. The audience wants the goal to be clearly defined so they can feel involved emotionally with the main character as he pursues the goal.

OBSTACLES

If a story is about the struggle of the main character to solve the pivotal problem, then there had better be interesting struggles. Great obstacles make great stories. If there had been no government agents in *ET*, then getting ET home would have simply been a story about contacting outer space. What are we going to worry about? Walt Disney said that it wasn't Snow White that made him rich, it was the witch. If there is no obstacle to rise up against, there can be no hero.

Conflict is drama, and drama is conflict. Problems, conflict and obstacles make the story engine run. If you find your character in a scene with no problems, invent problems—quickly—or your scene will grind to a halt.

THE OR-ELSE FACTOR

The main character must solve the problem, "or else." The or-else factor is the consequence. Elliot has to get ET home, or else ET will become a government experiment and may never see his home again. The father in *Lorenzo's Oil* must find a cure for his son's disease, or else his son will die.

CLOCK

The "clock" as a story element simply means a time limit placed on the main character to achieve his or her goal. She has to solve the problem by a certain time, or else. The father in *Lorenzo's Oil* knows that his son has six months to live unless a cure is found. He has to find a cure within six months, or else his son will die. The "clock" is not meant to be used in every story. Use it when it works.

LOCATION

I mention "location" as a story element because it's one of the first things the audience wants to know. Does it take place in a small Southern town (like *To Kill a Mockingbird*) or in New York City (like just about all of Woody Allen's movies)? The audience wants to know.

These story elements are the basic "gears" that make the story engine turn. Let's take a look, now, at how we can mix and match these elements to create a story.

If you want to grow a strong oak tree, start with an acorn that contains the necessary elements to grow a strong tree.

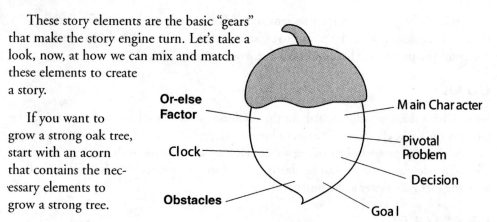

If you want to grow a strong screenplay, start with the necessary story elements.

MIX AND MATCH ELEMENTS TO SPARK A STORY

When I was a kid, I had a chemistry set. Ink did not exist in the chemistry set by itself. You had to take three different "chemicals," mix them together, and, suddenly, you had ink. The same thing is true for a story.

Some new writers think that when they're looking for a story, they're looking for a plot. There is no such thing as a "plot" out there all by itself. "Plots" do not grow in nature. They grow from a combination of story elements.

Ideally, the plot is character in action. A character takes action to solve the problem. The action that follows is the plot. The main character creates the plot through her struggle to reach her goal. What happens is the plot. But, remember, you create the main character and the obstacles, so—the truth is—you also create the plot.

How do we mix elements to make a story? There are lots of ways. One is to start with what you've got.

1) You could start with a character and add a problem.

   Have you ever seen an interesting character walking down the street and wondered about his life? What did he do for a living? Was he married? What was his childhood like? What were his dreams? Does he have any left? In your imagining, give him a problem and see what he does with it.

2) You could start with a problem and add a character.

   Let's say we wanted to deal with the problem of peer pressure to use alcohol. Start with that problem, then add a character that you think fits with that problem. How do you want the story to end? Do you want the main character to give in to peer pressure? Or, do you want the main character to find the courage to stand up to peer pressure? Pick the kind of character that you want, to give you the ending that you want, and you have a story in the making.

3) You could start with a theme.

   Let's say that you believe that "forgiveness works." That's a message you want to communicate through a story. Fine. Now you have to find a problem and a character who will help you communicate that message. Be careful with "theme." Nobody wants to be lectured. Tell a good story. Let the message emerge on its own. If you make the audience care about your character, they will—naturally—care about the message that character embraces. One of my screen writing teachers, who later created *Dr. Quinn: Medicine Woman*, used to say, "In through the heart, out through the head." Make the audience care first, then, later, they will think about what you were trying to say.

4) Even though "plot" does not exist on its own, you can start with an event, and build a story around that event by creating a main character and a pivotal problem to go with that event. Years ago, in the small town where I grew up, a meteorite shot from the heavens, crashed through a woman's roof and smacked her right on her rear end, making her the only human being in the history of the world to ever be hit by a falling star. This was unique, colorful and exciting, but it wasn't a story. It was an event. When I moved to Hollywood, I created a main character and a problem to go with that event and sold it to Twentieth Century Fox.

A story can be born from any combination of elements as long as you add in the main character, the pivotal problem, the decision and the obstacles. I have to tell you, though, a real fertile place to look for stories is in problems.

PROBLEMS ARE A WRITER'S BEST FRIEND

Everybody has problems. Might as well have fun with them by turning them into stories. Do you have a problem from your past that bugs you? Would you like to go back and fix it, now, through a story? When I was a senior in high school we lost the last football game of the year to the cross-town rivals. I never had a chance to play another game, to "fix" that loss. Losing that game always bugged me. Years later, I decided to create a character who would make the decision to rally his old team together and go back and replay that game. I sold it to Disney.

When I work with students to create a screenplay, we talk about the problems teens wrestle with in their everyday lives. Peer pressure. Parental pressure. Pressure to use alcohol. These problems are fertile ground for growing a story. One girl was upset because her father wanted to keep a pistol in the house. She thought that was wrong. A boy in the class thought it was right. They disagreed. If two students in your class disagree, use it. Disagreement is perfect for a story conference. Disagreement is conflict. Conflict is drama. Out of that "disagreement," we created a fantastic story dealing with the controversy of keeping a gun in the house. I was proud of those kids. Hollywood screenwriters could not have done better.

One of the boys in the class was in the high school in-crowd. He felt wrong, though, because certain members of his "in-crowd" were cruel to a person they considered to be a loser. How could he reconcile being a good person with being the member of a group who was cruel to another? Out of his struggle, we created a story about a boy who grew emotionally and came to realize he did not have to win the approval of the in-crowd. He was fine on his own.

If you can find a problem that people care about in their hearts, then you can create a story by adding a main character, a decision and obstacles.

When creating a story, you'll come to see that there are story "beats" that work well within the three-act structure. I want you to understand how and where the story elements we've discussed so far fit into the three-act structure.

THE THREE-ACT STRUCTURE

The three-act structure has been around a long time, since the ancient Greeks and Romans. It works. You do not have to be a slave to it, but—in order to teach these basics—we need to talk about the three-act structure.

In the diagram below, you'll notice that act two is twice as long as act one and act three. This is an example. Your act one could be shorter, or longer, depending upon the needs of your story. But, generally speaking, act two is longer than act one or act three.

When the decision to solve the problem is made, the goal is born. The line from the decision to the goal is the story line, or the spine of the story.

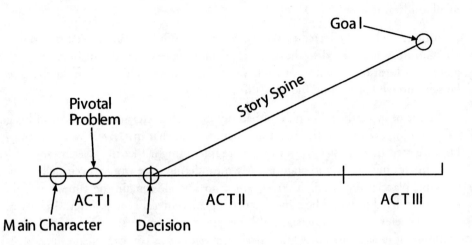

ACT ONE

Early in the story, we establish our location. We let the audience know where the story takes place.

Soon, we meet the main character. The main character may not have encountered the pivotal problem yet, but it usually works well to meet the character when he or she is caught up in the midst of a problem. Seeing how a character deals with a problem reveals a lot about character.

The main character encounters the pivotal problem of the story. He may not make a decision to solve that problem right away. When you encounter problems, do you immediately make a decision to solve them? Many of us avoid our problems at first, because problems are difficult. Who wants trouble?

Finally, though, the heat is turned up, and the main character realizes that she has to solve that problem. For reasons of the heart, for survival, for the survival of someone she loves, or for any number of reasons, the main character makes the decision to solve the problem. The moment the main character makes that decision, the goal is born and act one ends.

ACT TWO

Act two deals with the main character, struggling against the obstacles, in relentless pursuit of his goal.

He moves toward solving the problem, then suffers set-backs. He rallies his forces and moves closer to solving the problem, only to suffer an even greater set-back.

I have said that the story is about the main character's pursuit of the goal. That's true. But that's not the only thing it can be about. We want to have fun with the story. As long as the main character never loses sight of the goal, he can get himself mixed up in all kinds of messes.

Alfred Hitchcock referred to the goal as the "McGuffin." He agreed that the "McGuffin" was required so the audience would know where the main character was going, but he also felt that what really mattered was the trouble the main character got herself into while pursuing the McGuffin.

In one of my early screenplays, I had my main character in hot pursuit of his goal. After reading the first draft, one of my mentors said that my "river" was too straight. He suggested that my story would be more interesting if I let the river meander, discovering interesting nooks and crannies. My meandering river would, eventually, end up at the same place as my "straight" river, so the goal would remain the same, but if the river meandered it would be a more satisfying and entertaining journey. As long as your main character does not lose sight of his goal (or give up pursuit of that goal), he can find himself in as many crazy, meandering, situations as you can dream up.

THE LOW OF LOWS

Throughout act two, the obstacles must get bigger. The main character overcomes the obstacles. The obstacles overcome the main character. The main character battles them back.

Finally, though, the main character encounters a problem that it looks as if he will not be able to solve. This is the "low of lows." There is a pause at this point in the story. It appears that the main character is defeated. It appears that, now, because of what has happened, there is no way the main character can reach the goal.

The main character takes this moment to stop, think and assess the situation. In this moment of reflection, something that has been planted in the story earlier occurs to the main character. Maybe a bit of information—something that didn't mean anything earlier, but it does now. This idea that has occurred to him, could be the solution to the problem. There's no guarantee, but it just might work.

Armed now with this new information, the main character scrambles back into the story. He has one more shot at solving the problem. It's now or never.

In *ET*, the space creature was very sick. The children told their mother. She called the authorities. ET was caught, but even worse, he was dying. This was the low of lows. It looked, for certain, as if there would be no way for Elliot to achieve his goal of helping ET return safely home.

With ET dying, the authorities allowed Elliot one last chance to say good-bye. As Elliot said good-bye, ET died. Elliot was sad. But, then, at this lowest of all moments, Elliot saw the flower bloom. He knew that meant that ET was still alive because the flower had been associated earlier in the movie with "bringing back to life." The seeds had been planted along the way. Elliot grabbed onto that information and climbed back into the story. His goal was clear: Get ET to the mother ship before the authorities could stop them.

This low of lows indicates the end of act two. When the main character discovers the seeds of the solution, he grabs a metaphorical rope and swings into action for one last, fully committed effort. As he swings out on that rope, he lands right in the beginning of act three.

ACT THREE

The main character leaps into act three, more determined than ever now. He climbs a high mountain. But the obstacles, now, are more determined than ever, too. They knock him back into a valley. The main character claws his way up the next mountain. Battling through these "ups" and "downs," the main character finally reaches the climactic scene. In the climactic scene, the main character either achieves the goal, or he does not achieve the goal. (He either solves the problem, or he does not solve the problem.)

Here's something to remember: The story begins when the problem begins. The story ends when the problem is solved.

Drama is conflict, and conflict is drama. If you don't have a problem, you don't have a story. The audience will allow you a reasonable amount of time to introduce your location and your characters. Soon, though, they want to see the main character meet the problem. That is the point where the story, the drama, begins. The climax, where that problem is resolved, one way or the other, is where the story ends.

The audience will allow you one final story beat after the pivotal problem is resolved. It's called the denouement, a French word that means, "The final disentangling of the intricacies of a plot." If you try to add more story than the denouement, after the pivotal problem is solved, you're going to run into trouble. When the pivotal problem is solved, the story is over. Let it go.

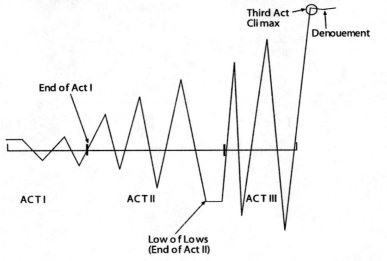

You may say, with all these dramatic "ups" and "downs," that this is the three-act structure for an action movie. This three-act structure applies to an action movie and, equally, to a character story. In the action movie, these "ups" and "downs" represent physical danger. In a character story, the "ups" and "downs" represent emotional danger. When the father in *Lorenzo's Oil* moves closer toward achieving his goal in act three, the threat of his son's illness also increases. The son's time is running out.

We've talked about the elements that mix together to build a story. We know where they fit in the three-act structure. Let's mix them all together and make a story.

THE STORY CONFERENCE

Before we begin, let's arm ourselves with idea-catching tools—a pad of yellow "stickies" and several pencils. Gather around a table. There can be three students there, or twelve. It doesn't matter. The more the merrier. Our goal is to "spitball" ideas and come up with a story. By this time, every student should have at least some understanding of the basic story elements and how they fit into the three-act structure.

We're going to come up with all kinds of wonderful, wild ideas in a story conference. Anything goes. In order to do that, we're going to create an "Idea Bowl."

You all know how to find the "Big Dipper." You just look up at the heavens and connect the stars to form a pattern. To draw an "Idea Bowl," you connect all the story elements.

To draw an Idea Bowl,
learn this rhyme:

Main character, problem,
Decision, goal.
They make a great big
Idea bowl.

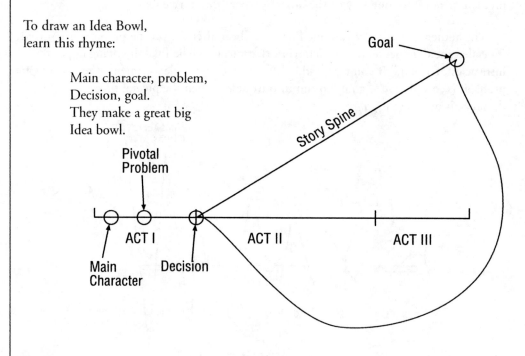

Start on the left and connect main character to problem to decision, then shoot up to the right to connect with the "goal," located at the third act climax. Then loop around, back to decision. By connecting these story elements, you've made a powerful bowl, perfect for catching story ideas.

Fill this bowl with story ideas—whatever pops into your mind. Worry about the order they come in later.

THERE ARE NO BAD IDEAS

There is no such thing as a bad idea. Coming up with ideas is a delicate process. It's like pulling a red thread out of a bail of hay. If you pull too hard, you will break the thread—and there's no getting it back once it's broken. Kids are capable of coming up with creative, smart, exciting and fresh ideas. But if someone tells them their idea is bad, they will pull their heads back into their shells quicker than you can say "turtle." When it comes to creating a story, there are no bad ideas—because all ideas lead to good ideas. I once saw a documentary about Nobel-Prize-winning scientist Linus Pauling. In the movie, his grandson asked him, "Granddad, where do good ideas come from?" Linus Pauling smiled. His eyes bugged a little in excitement, then he said, "By having lots of bad ones."

If you still have trouble with kids coming up with ideas, because they're afraid of looking silly, play the "bad idea" contest. Set a timer on three minutes. Challenge them to come up with as many "bad ideas" as they can in three minutes. And they had better be bad! They'll jump right into that contest. And who knows? You might just discover the spark of a terrific idea in the "bad idea" contest. In any event, your pump is primed now. The kids have played the game. It's not so scary. It's time to make up a story.

A REAL LIVE STORY CONFERENCE

What I've decided to do is take you through a real-time, this-is-actually-how-it-is story conference. We're all gathered around a table, making idea notes on yellow stickies and tossing them into the idea bowl. As we come up with ideas, we will see them begin to form into a story. Out of that story, we will create an outline. Out of that outline, we will begin to write a screenplay.

I have no idea where this story will go. We'll make it up "on the fly." You scared? That's perfect! I'm scared too. All writers are scared before they begin. But what's there to be scared of? There's no such thing as a bad idea. Smile and dive in.

Where do we start?

As I have said, over and over again, one of the best places to start is with problems. But, first, let's deal with reality. What "givens" do we have? Let's say that we know we are creating this story so we can make a movie at the special day-long class that comes up in two weeks. Okay. Where's the class going to be? It's going to be at the school. So we know we need to make up a story we can shoot somewhere around the school. Okay. Who do we have to act? The members of the class. They're perfect because they're all genius actors!

Do you see what we're doing? Instead of just coming up with a story, we're tailor-making a story to work with what we have. If the basis of a story is a problem, let's talk about problems.

In the course of our conversation, one student says he may not be coming to the class. He may have to stay home and take care of his rebellious little brother. We sense sibling rivalry. Now there's a problem we can all relate to. We talk about it. The group seems excited. It's a problem they all seem to understand. Let's "spitball" that problem and see where it takes us.

Here's one approach that seems realistic: Instead of a class the big brother is supposed to go to, it's a party. The big brother wants to go to the party. The little brother wants to go too, but the big brother doesn't want him to go. The big brother tells little brother that he's a nerd. He would only embarrass him if he brought him to the party.

Little brother has a problem. He wants to go to the party, but he does not have permission to go.

Little brother makes a decision to solve that problem. (This decision is a turning point in the story. It sets our main character into action.)

Little brother finds out that the party starts at 7:00 p.m. It's 6:00 p.m. now. Little brother decides he will sneak into the school and "stow away." His plan is that, by the time they find him, the party will be well under way, and he will be allowed to stay.

Little brother sneaks into the school and hides in a closet. Seven o'clock passes. Little brother sneaks out of the closet, wondering where everybody is. He pulls out the party flier to take a look. On close inspection, he discovers he's come to the wrong school. The party was scheduled for the school across the street!

Okay. That's fun. The little brother discovers he's gone to the wrong school. But that's not enough for a story. We need more. How will we find it?

Simple. We've got to get the little brother into more trouble. We have to keep conflict going in order to have a story. The story is the main character trying to solve the problem. If we don't have a problem, we don't have a story.

So what could our problem be now?

The kid is in the school alone. What if he went over to the door to leave, only to discover that he's locked in? Okay. Let's think logically (because the audience thinks logically—and they're going to expect the story to follow some kind of logic). What would you do if you were locked in? I'd admit my mistake and call my parents. But this kid's parents aren't home. It doesn't matter. He'll call the police. He's in a fix. He tries to call the police, but the phone is dead. (We need to manufacture the problem of the dead phone to keep our main character in trouble. If he calls the police, they will let him out. The problem will be solved, and the story will be over. Who wants that?!)

Let's go back and see what we can do to complicate the telephone. Notice I said, "go back." We find we need something to keep little brother from calling, but we can't just add it, out of nowhere. We need to go back in the story and "plant" something that will make the dead telephone believable. How about a thunder storm? That would knock out a phone. Write "plant thunder storm" on a stickie and toss it into the idea bowl.

Now we have little brother locked inside the school. Plus, the phone is dead. What's he gonna do? What would you do? You'd climb out the window? Okay, try that.

Little brother starts out the window. Just as he does, though, he runs into two villainous cat burglars!

Cat burglars? Where did cat burglars come from?

They came from our imagination. We have to keep our main character in trouble, or the story will be over. Cat burglars sound like fun trouble to me. Put it in the story bowl and let's see where it goes.

Little brother opens the window and starts climbing out, only to discover two cat burglars climbing in.

But, wait a minute. Doesn't it seem a little convenient for cat burglars to come along right now? It's too easy. The audience won't believe it. Plus, if little brother sees two people climbing in, he won't necessarily know they're cat burglars. If he perceives no threat, we have no problem. But if little brother knows there are cat burglars in the neighborhood, it makes it twice as much fun now. That means we need to go back in the story and plant the cat burglars. That's the way these story conferences work. Back and forth. Move forward. Find out what you need. Go back and plant it.

Remember when little brother was sneaking into the school? Let's say that, during that scene, we saw the principal talking to a salesman about a burglar alarm. Seems the school had, just that day, had a burglar alarm installed. The principal exclaims that they need the burglar alarm. Seems there are two notorious cat burglars in the neighborhood that the police have been unable to catch.

Now the cat burglars are set up. They're "planted." When we meet them later, we "pay them off."

In Hollywood movies, this kind of information is called exposition—information the audience needs to know in order to understand the story. Sometimes exposition can be deadly. You want a scene to be alive with conflict, not dead with information. One of the tricks to writing exposition is to deliver the boring facts while something else is going on that the audience will worry about. If the principal tells the burglar alarm man about the cat burglars while little brother is about to trip over the hat rack in the background, then we're worried about little brother getting caught—and we're not bored with hearing nothing but exposition.

Let's go back to where we left off—the cat burglars are sneaking in the window. Little brother sees them. He can't believe his eyes. It's the cat burglars! If he tries to climb out, they'll grab him. He does the only thing he knows to do. He runs back into the school and hides.

But wait a minute, we're writing this story to fit the members of our class. What about making one of the cat burglars a girl? Cat-burglar woman? We love it. Put that yellow stickie in the idea bowl.

Little brother watches the cat burglars as they stalk around the school. "Whoever left that window open for us, sure was nice," one of the burglars laughs. Little brother gulps. He had just opened that window to crawl out. The cat burglars are inside the school, and it's his fault.

Little brother looks down the hall, toward the burglar alarm. If he is going to seek to solve his problem by pulling that alarm, we'll need to plant more information. We have to know that pulling the alarm would have an effect. So, let's say that, in the earlier scene, between the principal and the burglar alarm salesperson, we add this information: The burglar alarm is not yet fully operational. It won't work tonight. But if someone actually pulled the alarm, that would alert the police. But then they laugh, who would be nutty enough to break into the school and pull the alarm?

Little brother sneaks down the hall, toward the burglar alarm. He's just about to reach for the alarm when he trips over that same pesky hat rack. The cat burglars hear the commotion, spot our hero and give chase.

Because of the direction the cat burglars are coming from, our hero can't make it to the burglar alarm.

He turns and runs through the school. The doors are locked. He can't get out. They pursue him.

What are we writers gonna do?

To figure out what we're going to do, let's go back to the basics. A story is about a main character who sets about to solve a problem. Our hero definitely has a problem, and he'd better solve it, or he's going to be "cat burglar stew."

Here's an idea! What if cat-burglar woman got her name because she always carries her cat whenever she burglarizes. That's her weak point. Cat-burglar woman is mean, but she loves her cat—and carries it tucked away under her cat-burglar coat. How can adding this cat help our main character solve this problem? Let's spitball and see.

Trouble is a writer's best friend. How can you get a cat in trouble? The general belief is that cats are afraid of dogs. Where could we come up with a dog? We don't want the dog to come out of nowhere, so let's go back and plant one. (This is the way a real story conference works. Come up with ideas and add them to the story. If they need to be planted, go back and find a believable place to plant them.)

Let's say that the principal found a stray dog. During the conversation about the burglar alarm, the principal mentions to the alarm salesman that he had hoped this dog would be a "burglar alarm," because the principal doesn't want to take the dog to the pound. They decide to leave the dog in the school that night because of the burglars. The principal knows the dog likes to chase cats. "Maybe," they say laughingly "that means he'll chase a cat burglar." While this information is being communicated, it's important that we get the feeling that little brother overhears it. If he's going to act on this information later, we have to get the feeling that it's "planted in his head" now.

Let's spitball and see how we can do that.

There's the scene where little brother sees the cat burglars sneaking in and runs to hide. Let's say he hides in a nearby closet. When cat-burglar woman sneaks in, she stumbles and almost falls. She stops and looks at something hidden under her coat. She begins to talk to it. As she does, we realize she is talking to her cat. Did her stumble scare the itty bitty kitty? Cat-burglar woman promises her cat that she would never let anything hurt it. Little brother may not think much about that cat now, but it's planted in his mind (and the mind of the audience) that cat-burglar woman will do anything to protect that cat.

Let's come back to where we left our story earlier. Little brother was running through the church with the two cat burglars in hot pursuit. As they give chase, now, he happens to run into a room.

In that room, he finds himself face to face with the principal's dog. Just then, little brother remembers the information that he overheard earlier—that this dog loves to chase cats. A light bulb turns on for little brother. If he can lure the cat burglars into this room, the dog will chase the cat, keeping the cat burglars at bay, allowing little brother time to pull the burglar alarm. He's not sure it will work, but it's the only shot he has. He tells the dog to "stay!" Then sneaks back into the hall, determined to lure the cat-burglars into his trap.

Something occurs to me at this point in the story. We haven't seen the older brother. What's he doing? He's supposed to be at the party. Through our writer's imaginations, we go to the party and find big brother there, doing his best to be cool. A girl asks him where his little brother is. Big brother says, off-handedly, "Probably sitting at home, living his boring life." Off that remark, we find—

Little brother, back in the other school, waving his arms madly, attracting the attention of the cat burglars. The plan works. They spot him and give chase.

It's a wild chase through the hallways. Finally, little brother takes his one big chance and, making sure they're watching, ducks into the school library. If his plan works, the dog will corner the cat burglars, giving little brother time to run down the hall and pull the alarm. If his plan doesn't work, he'll be trapped and suffer cat-burglar-consequences.

When the cat burglars see little brother go into the library, they laugh with sinister glee, commenting that there are no windows in the library. The boy will not be able to escape. They will make short work of him.

They enter the library, find our hero and move toward him, threatening. Little brother looks to the dog for help, but the dog just sits there.

Just when it looks like our hero is doomed, the dog sniffs the air, then, suddenly, barks at cat burglar woman. She cowers in the corner, holding her cat close. The other cat burglar stands alongside her, keeping the dog at bay.

Little brother runs down the hall and pulls the alarm.

Across the street, at the party, we overhear the sound of police sirens. A kid who we met earlier at the party runs up to big brother and others, shouting that the cat burglars have been caught. Some kid caught them single-handedly. The kids from the party hurry toward the school.

Back at little brother's school, the cat burglars are led away. The big kids from the party look on, awestruck, as they overhear others proclaim that this kid who caught the cat burglars will be the town hero.

Just then, the kid who caught the cat burglars turns and big brother sees who it is. It's his little brother! He stares in disbelief while little brother smiles back. Maybe he's not quite such a geek after all.

Just then, the kids from the party walk over to little brother, introduce themselves, and invite him to their party. Little brother accepts, under one condition: They let him bring his dog. Seems the principal let him have the dog. He's already given it a name—*Party Animal*. The big kids love it. His dog is welcome. (Note: To make this dog pay off, go back to the opening scene [where little brother argued with big brother] and plant the dog. Maybe the little brother said that he wanted to go to the party to make new friends—and the big brother sneered, "Get a Dog." See how going back and planting the dog makes the dog "pay off" in a more powerful way?!)

As little brother starts across toward the party, with his new friends, he looks back at his big brother and signals to him that it's okay for him to come along too.

THE END

Congratulations! We just wrote a story—made it up right there on the spot. We didn't sharpen a hundred pencils and wait for the mood to strike. We built a story, using the basic elements:

1) A problem. Sibling rivalry.

2) We decided which sibling would have the problem. (The little brother.)

3) We defined the problem. (Little brother wants to go to the party, but big brother won't let him.)

4) We had our main character make a decision to overcome his problem by reaching a specific goal. (He'll "stow away" and go to the party anyway.)

5) We put our main character in the location where we knew we would be shooting the movie. In that location, we had him work toward his goal. As he worked toward his goal, we gave him problems he had to solve, "or else."

6) If we added a story point that did not seem motivated, we went back and "planted" information—so that story point would seem believable later.

7) We created obstacles that grew more and more threatening as the story progressed.

8) When forced into a desperate situation, we created a way for the main character to solve his own problems. (In other words, nothing came along and solved the problem for him.)

9) The main character grew emotionally in the process, learning that he is actually a pretty cool guy, no matter what his older brother might think.

We've spitballed a story. It's all on yellow stickies in the idea bowl. Take those stickies out now, and put them in the order that they come in the story. Once you have them in order, write an outline.

An outline is simply the "steps" of what happens. Like this:

"Party Animal"
(step outline)

1) Big brother prepares to go to the party at the local school. Little brother wants to go. Big brother is the one who was invited, and he won't let little brother go, saying he would embarrass him. Seems the family just moved to town. Little brother doesn't have any friends. If he goes to the party, little brother hopes he might make some friends. Big brother tells him that, if he wants a friend, to get a dog. Then, he leaves.

Little brother reads the party invitation. The party starts at 7:00 p.m. It's only 6:00 now. Little brother decides to go to the school, sneak in and stow away. Once they realize he's there, they will allow him to stay. Since he's new to town, he's never been to this school before. He checks the address. The school is on Elm Street.

2) The school principal's office. The principal and the burglar alarm salesman talk. The purpose of the scene is to plant information about the burglar alarm, the cat burglars and the dog—while little brother sneaks in, in the background.

In each step of the outline, it is sufficient to simply write the purpose of the scene. That provides you with enough information to know what happens in that scene. It also forces you to get to the point, without including information that does not matter at the outline stage.

When writing the outline, if you have a new idea that you think makes the story better, use it. Stories are not written, they're rewritten. Talk about the outline in your story conference. Make changes. When you don't know what else to change, it's time to write the screenplay.

WRITING THE SCREENPLAY

So much of writing the screenplay is getting ready, coming up with the story, creating an outline. If you have a strong outline, writing the screenplay goes a lot easier.

To write a screenplay, take the information from our story conference, write an outline, then write your own screenplay. See what you can do with it. And remember, the story can change in the process of writing. There's a magic that comes with the heat of writing. If the magic tells you to take the story in a different direction, do it. The secret to writing is writing. Discover that secret.

SCREENPLAY FORMAT

A screenplay is written in a specific format. You don't have to stick with this format. If you want to scribble your script on a legal pad, that's fine. But if you want to know what the format looks like, I'll put the first scene of the movie into screenplay format.

INT. BEDROOM—DAY ⟵——————————— **SLUG LINE**

A teenage boy's bedroom. Clothes everywhere. Posters of sports figures. There's a mirror on the wall. THE CAMERA ADJUSTS to discover a seventeen-year-old boy, BIG BROTHER, staring in the mirror, combing his hair.

From somewhere in the room, we hear the off-screen voice of another boy, LITTLE BROTHER.

                    LITTLE BROTHER ⟵——————— **CHARACTER NAME**
          Mirror, mirror on the wall.
          Who's the coolest of them all? ⟵—— **DIALOGUE**

The CAMERA ADJUSTS to discover Little Brother, twelve years old, sitting on the edge of the bed, staring up at Big Brother. Big Brother looks back disdainfully, then—

                    BIG BROTHER
          I am.

                 LITTLE BROTHER
          Excuse me. I almost forgot.

Then Little Brother notices a flier sitting on
the bed. Big letters proclaim "Party." He picks
it up, studying it.

                 LITTLE BROTHER
                  (continuing)
          Why can't I go to this party?   **DESCRIPTION**

                    BIG BROTHER
          Because they invited me, not
          you.

                 LITTLE BROTHER
          That doesn't mean I can't go.
             (standing, demonstrating)
          You could say, "This is my
          little brother. We just moved to
          town. He wants to make friends,
          too."

                    BIG BROTHER
          If I took you, you'd probably
          just embarrass me.

                 LITTLE BROTHER
          I'll act really cool. They'll
          think I'm at least sixteen
          (backing down, then—)
          ...or fifteen.

                    BIG BROTHER
          You're not going, geek.

Big brother brushes his hair one last time,
starts away. Little brother shouts after him.

> LITTLE BROTHER
> The school is a public
> institution open to public
> citizens. I might just go
> anyway.

But big brother keeps walking. Then little
brother shouts desperately.

> LITTLE BROTHER
> I need to find a friend.

> BIG BROTHER
> Get a dog!

Then big brother is gone, disappearing around
the corner.

Little brother wanders over and picks up the
party flier. He reads, mumbling to himself.

> LITTLE BROTHER
> "All welcome"
>   (he looks into the
>   mirror)
> "All."
>   (pointing to himself)
> That includes you.

He looks back at the flier. It says: "Party
starts at 7:00."

> LITTLE BROTHER
>   (reading to himself)
> Starts at seven.

```
He looks over at the digital clock. It's 6:00
now. Little Brother looks back at his own image
in the mirror and smiles. This boy has an idea.
And he's about to act on it.

                                            CUT TO:
```

SCREENPLAY "STUFF"   TRANSITION

The definition of a scene is whenever you change time or location. The scene that takes place in the house, between the two brothers, is one scene. When we cut to the school, that would be a different scene, because of the change of location. If we had stayed in the house but cut to, say, the little brother watching television an hour later, that would constitute a different scene because of the change in time.

The slug line tells us the location, whether it's interior or exterior, day or night.

"Description" tells us what we see on the screen. Watch the movie in your mind. What do you see? Write it down. That's "description."

The purpose of dialogue is to provide information, reveal character or advance the plot. When you write dialogue, ask yourself later, when editing, if your dialogue fulfills one or more of those purposes.

Voice-over narration is a good way to provide exposition, or information the audience needs to know in order to follow the story. In Frank Capra's *It's A Wonderful Life*, the movie opens with the heavens talking with an angel named Clarence. That voice-over provides information so that we can understand the story. Use voice-over, but don't use it all the time. It can become a crutch, keeping you from learning how to handle exposition through dialogue and description.

A FEW MORE CHARACTER NOTES

You know more than you think you know. That's especially true of character. You know that there are different sides to your own character. You have a generous side and a selfish side, a courageous side and a worry-wart side. Every character lives inside you somewhere. The thing to keep in mind when writing a screenplay is that every character has a dominant character trait. This dominant trait will reveal itself in the midst of conflict. How a character reacts to a problem reveals volumes about who he or she is. Is he brave? Is he petty? Throw him a problem and see.

One note about "the bad guy" character. In the foreword to his play *Blues For Mister Charley*, James Baldwin reminded us that no man is evil in his own eyes. When you write a bad guy, realize that he has a goal too. He probably thinks he has a worthy goal. In fact, he probably believes in his goal as much as your hero believes in her goal.

Remember, if you don't have a strong villain, you can't have a strong hero. If you are able to keep that in mind, you'll be able to write believable three-dimensional antagonists.

DEUS EX MACHINA

In the days of the ancient Greek and Roman plays, they often had the gods, like Zeus and Athena, drop down out of nowhere to solve the third-act problem. The main character did not solve the problem. *Deus ex machina* meant, literally, "god from a machine."

That won't work today. The audience wants to see the main character solve the problem through his or her own efforts. That doesn't mean the main character can't pray, seeking guidance, wisdom, and strength to solve the problem. That's fine. But, if a bad guy is chasing your good guy and suddenly, out of nowhere, a tornado drops down and whisks the bad guy away, that won't work. The audience wants the emotional satisfaction that the main character solved the problem through his or her own faith, struggle and effort.

HOMEWORK

Watch *ET*. See if you can find the end of act one, the end of act two, and the third-act climax. Can you identify the main character and the goal? Look for ways the writer worked exposition into the dialogue, without it seeming like exposition. Notice how the writer introduces characters. Can you find the low of lows? If so, what are the seeds of the solution? Did the main character change or grow emotionally? Was the pivotal problem solved or not solved?

WRAPPING UP

Finally, and this may be the most important writing lesson of all, do not edit yourself when writing. Once you start writing, write! Have fun with it. Sing your story. There is a little scowly-faced critic who lives inside all of us and tells us that what we're doing is no good. Don't listen to him. He doesn't know anything anyway. If he were smart, he'd have a better job than sitting around bothering us all the time. Whenever he raises his head and tries to speak, tell him you'll be glad to listen to him later. Then go back to your work. Write now. There will be plenty of time for second-guessing later.

THE SECRET OF WRITING

The secret of writing is writing. That's where the real magic happens. So, go. Start writing. Discover that secret. And maybe even tell some truth about the human spirit.

Preproduction

My favorite film director, Frank Capra, who directed such masterpieces as *It's A Wonderful Life*, *Mr. Smith Goes to Washington*, and *It Happened One Night*, believed that the key to good production is good preproduction. A simple way to define preproduction is "planning." When building a house, the materials, crew and schedule are based upon the blueprint. When building a movie, the equipment, crew and schedule are based upon the script. Hollywood has, over the years, developed time-honored systems for planning, or "prepping," a movie. We'll cover the basics.

By the time you're ready to begin preproduction, you should have finished your screenplay. Before you type "final draft," though, let's deal with locations and casting. We don't want to "lock down," or finalize, our script until we see if locations or casting may cause changes.

LOCATIONS

The first requirement of a location is obvious: Does it look right for the scene? However, there are other important aspects to consider:

1) Electricity. If you'll need electricity for lights, does this location have electricity? If you're shooting in, say, a barn where there is no electricity, can you run a cable from a nearby house?

2) Sunlight. If the sun is your major source of light, you'll want to consider where the sun will be at the time of day you're shooting at this location. (If the location is a deck on the eastern side of a house, it will be bright in the morning and shady in the late afternoon.)

3) Noise. If there is noise at the location, you'll want it to be noise you can control, like an air conditioner you can turn off. If you're not recording dialogue at this location, then noise should not be a concern. Beware of locations with noise you cannot control—like the loud sounds around a highway or an airport.

4) Crowd control. Let's say your scene calls for a shot through the front window of a store. It will ruin your shot if the camera sees people, outside, staring at the camera. Try to pick a location where members of your crew can have permission to stand on the sidewalk and politely stop sidewalk traffic during your "take." The store manager may grant you that permission. Or, you may need to get permission from your friendly local policeman.

5) Availability. Once you find a location that is right for your movie, go to the owner of the property and explain your project. People usually want to help. Some, though, will have at least a few concerns. The property owner may ask for a "release," relieving him from liability should somebody get hurt. What if your crew breaks their favorite lamp? Will you clean up when you leave? What's the best time to use the location? These details must be discussed and agreed upon. When you have reached an understanding, it's good to put it in writing. (You may download a sample "property release" from our web site.)

CASTING

Casting is simply finding the right person to play the part. In addition to acting ability, you want a person who is motivated and mature enough to show up at the right place at the right time and know his or her lines.

Actors can be students, people from your church, scout troop or local theater group. You might know a person who has no acting experience, but looks right for the part. This is called "casting to type." Just because he may never have had acting experience before, doesn't mean he can't act. Let him audition for the part. If you feel that he has a sense of drama, give him a shot.

An audition could be as simple as going through the school, asking the "right looking" people to show up that afternoon to be in a movie. Or, you can have more formal casting sessions, asking people to show up at a certain place at a certain time to audition for the part.

When asking someone to audition, consider the appearance, age and demeanor of the person. Does he look like the character you had in mind when you wrote the script? If so, you need to see if he has a sense of drama. When he comes in to audition, give him one of his scenes. Allow him time to prepare. Once prepared, give him a chance to read his part. When reading, does he have a sense of drama? Can he bring life to the part? If so, he may work. If not, keep looking. There is nothing worse than to get on location with an actor who simply cannot do the part. Some young children can be charming during the casting session, but—when it comes to production—they're too young to deliver lines properly. Don't find yourself in that situation. Make sure your actors can do the part before you get into production. (If a child is not right for the part, but you think rejection might hurt her feelings, check other places in the script, like a scene with extras, where she might fit in and feel included.)

If you cannot find the right person for the part, consider rewriting the part for the right person. Let's say your script calls for a seven-year-old boy, but you can't find one who can do the part. But you do have a nine-year-old girl who is terrific. Would it work to rewrite the part for the girl? Casting, like every other aspect of movie making, will not be perfect. Find the best person you can for the part and keep going.

If locations and casting bring about necessary changes in the script, make those changes, then "lock down" the script. "Locking" the script simply means that you declare that this is the draft you are going to use to shoot the movie and you "lock it down"— stop changing it. This does not mean you can't make changes later, in the process of shooting your movie. The actors and crew will have creative input during production, and you should always be open for creative changes. But, when you begin to schedule production, you must begin with a "locked" script.

Once you've made the final changes to the script, name the draft "Final Draft," then put a date on that draft. If you change the script later, call it "Revised Final Draft," then add the new date. The date on each draft will prevent later confusion if other drafts of the script happen to be around. All cast and crew should be working from the latest draft.

MAKING A PRODUCTION BOARD

Once you have your final draft, it's time to schedule your production. Using a pen, number each scene, to the left of each scene's slug line. Remember, the definition of a scene is any time you change time or location. Let's say your characters are inside a drugstore, having a conversation. At a certain point, you cut to the exterior of the drugstore, where the same characters walk out of the store, continuing their conversation. The interior of the drugstore and the exterior of the drug store would be two scenes, requiring two separate scene numbers. The requirements for the exterior, on the sidewalk, will be different than the requirements of the scene inside the drugstore. For the interior, you may need the two actors talking and another actor behind the counter. For the exterior, you may need a bicycle, extras and maybe an additional actor. Each separate scene, whenever we change location or time, must be numbered so that the requirements for each scene can be met and details do not fall between the cracks.

At this point, you have a final draft screenplay with a date on the cover page. Each scene in this script is numbered. It's now time to "break down" the script.

What this means, literally, is to break the script into its various components—props, locations, wardrobe, actors and extras. Hollywood identifies these various elements using different colored highlight markers. Reading through the script, you might highlight all props in yellow, all actors in green or all wardrobe in blue. Use your own color-coding system. The goal is to create a color-coded script in which your eye can easily spot each item that needs to be listed for preproduction. Once the script is color-coded, it's time to do the production board.

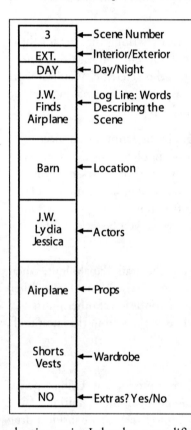

THE PRODUCTION BOARD

Hollywood uses production strips about a half inch wide, twelve inches long and about the thickness of poster paper. You can make your own production strips using typing paper.

The pertinent information from each numbered scene is written onto each strip so you can look at each strip and determine the actors, wardrobe and props needed for each scene. Actually, Hollywood uses codes on the strips because they have so much information. But, in our shorter movies, writing the information on the strip will be easier.

There is a space on the strip to tell if the scene takes place during day or night, interior or exterior. There is a space to note actors, props, wardrobe— and place for a "log line," a few words which describe the scene. Each strip represents one scene and should be assigned the number of the scene it represents. (Production strips are available on the web site. Feel free to use them, or design your own.)

This is not a perfect replica of a Hollywood production strip. It has been modified to better suit the needs of our productions.

Once the details have been transferred from the script to the strips, you will have a pile of strips. It's time to organize those strips into a shooting schedule.

THE SHOOTING SCHEDULE

Your shooting schedule is determined by many variables. There are days an actor is available and days that same actor is not available. You may also have to schedule around the availability of locations. Let's say that you have a scene inside a drugstore. The owner might be happy to let you shoot in his store, but not during business hours. There are scenes that require night shooting and scenes that require day shooting. There may be a scene that is written for night, but—if it's an interior (and the audience doesn't have to see outside) that scene can be scheduled anytime.

Common sense prevails when it comes to scheduling. If you're using an actor who works a full-time job, schedule her scenes on her day off. If you're shooting the interior of a store, schedule all those interiors at once. You don't want to shoot at a location, move to another location, then come back to the first location. Most students will be aware that we do not shoot scenes in the order that they come in the script. We shoot scenes out of sequence to keep production time to a minimum.

SCHEDULING THE PRODUCTION BOARD

First, group all the strips by location. Then, for each location, group the strips by interior or exterior, day or night. At this point, begin to order the strips, from left to right, depending upon which scene you want to shoot first, second, third, fourth and so on. The strips are "stand-alone" so you can move them around without having to cut and paste. Let's say that you have scheduled scene 7 for the first day of shooting. Later, you see it would be better to do scene 7 on day three. Just slide the strip for scene 7 out of the line-up and move it down to its new place in the ordered strips. Put as many strips together as you feel you can safely shoot on day one, then label the top of that section "Day 1," and so forth.

DAY 1				DAY 2			DAY 3			
7	8	3	1	9	5	2	11	10	4	6
EXT. DAY	EXT. DAY	EXT. DAY	EXT. DAY	EXT. DAY	EXT. DAY	EXT. DAY	EXT. DAY	EXT. DAY	EXT. DAY	EXT. DAY
I.V. Finds Airplane	I.V. Finds Airplane	I.V. Finds Airplane	I.V. Finds Airplane	I.V. Finds Airplane	I.V. Finds Airplane	I.V. Finds Airplane	I.V. Finds Airplane	I.V. Finds Airplane	I.V. Finds Airplane	I.V. Finds Airplane
Barn	Barn	Barn	Barn	Barn	Barn	Barn	Barn	Barn	Barn	Barn
I.V. Lydia Jessica	I.V. Lydia Jessica	I.V. Lydia Jessica	I.V. Lydia Jessica	I.V. Lydia Jessica	I.V. Lydia Jessica	I.V. Lydia Jessica	I.V. Lydia Jessica	I.V. Lydia Jessica	I.V. Lydia Jessica	I.V. Lydia Jessica
Airplane	Airplane	Airplane	Airplane	Airplane	Airplane	Airplane	Airplane	Airplane	Airplane	Airplane
Shorts Vests	Shorts Vests	Shorts Vests	Shorts Vests	Shorts Vests	Shorts Vests	Shorts Vests	Shorts Vests	Shorts Vests	Shorts Vests	Shorts Vests
YES	NO	YES	NO	NO	YES	NO	NO	YES	NO	YES

At this point, the strips are still on your table. When you have them in as good an order as you can get them (for now, anyway), it's time to create the "production board." Using push-pins, attach your strips to a cork board—in the order in which you had them on the table, with the first scheduled scene on the left, then adding strips (scenes) to the right. At the top of the group of strips you plan to shoot on the first day, put a short strip of paper that says "Day 1." Above the second day's group of strips, put another heading that says "Day 2," and so forth.

Once you have all the strips tacked to the cork board, you have your production board. It's time to make a production schedule.

THE PRODUCTION SCHEDULE

To make a production schedule, take the information from the strips and use it to type a schedule. If there are changes after the production schedule is typed, revise the schedule. With today's computers, revisions are not a problem. It's important that you make everyone aware of any changes through a revised production schedule. If you have an actress take a day off work and show up on the wrong day because she wasn't informed, you'll have one upset actress.

Scheduling is a balancing act. There will be times your location is available, but your actor is not. It's all part of the fun of movie making—creative problem-solving. Hollywood has to shoot movies without stopping. It would be too expensive to stop and start. But your smaller movie has the luxury of scheduling whatever works best for you. You might shoot three weekends in a row, or shoot every Sunday afternoon for six weeks. Do what works.

Let's review the steps used to schedule a production:

1) Finish script.

2) Find and secure locations.

3) Cast movie.

4) Rewrite script, if need be, based upon locations and casting.

5) "Lock" script and date it. Number scenes.

6) Break down script, using color codes.

7) Make production strips, one for each scene.

8) Organize production strips in the order in which you plan to shoot them.

9) Type and distribute production schedule.

At this point, your production is scheduled. But there's still preproduction for the various departments.

PRODUCTION DEPARTMENTS

A movie production is not a herd of people thundering off to shoot video footage and act. In Hollywood, production is done in departments. There's a Camera Department, a Sound Department, Make-up and Hair, etc. Each member of a movie crew has a specific job. The success of your production depends upon each person doing his or her job. That doesn't mean that a student has to be stuck in a job he doesn't want, but, sometimes, a student will have to do a job he may not want. He'll get to direct or shoot camera on the next movie. It will be up to you to decide the best way to share jobs so that the movie is completed and everyone gets to play.

1) Camera Department. The best choice for this department is the kid who is excited about cameras. Desire is the number one characteristic that determines success.

For the Camera Department to prepare for production, get the best camcorder you can get. Whatever you get will be fine. This program is about learning to make a movie, using equipment you already own or can borrow. It's not about learning how to buy expensive equipment.

Once you have a camera, it is the job of your Camera Person to learn how to use that camcorder. I am not going to teach you how to use your own camcorder. There are so many different camcorders out there, that would be impossible. Your Camera Person needs to read the manual that came with the camcorder and practice. How long do the batteries last? How long does it take to charge them? One perfect example of poor preproduction is to get out on location, away from electricity, and have the batteries go dead. If the batteries take four hours to recharge, you have lost the day. The student who is head of the Camera Department should experiment with every feature of that camcorder and practice and study the results of her practice sessions on her television at home.

The Camera Department is also in charge of lighting. Have one student, with a crew under him, be in charge of lighting. His job will be to gather the lights and grip equipment required to make the movie. Lighting deals with lights. Grip deals with things that control light, like reflectors, bounce card and stands for lights.

If the script calls for a dolly shot, it will be this person's job to find a wheel-chair, wheelbarrow, or grocery cart to carry the Camera Person during that dolly shot. But, until you have been through the script in a production meeting, you will not know what equipment, including lights, to gather.

2) Sound Department. Your camcorder will be your sound recorder. You will need microphones and something to help get the microphone out to the actor, like a cane pole or a long broom handle. Your Sound Person needs to get together with the Camera Person and practice. Production, with the clock ticking, is not the time to practice. Make sure your equipment is working properly during preproduction.

3) Art Department. Any set dressings you have, or props, will be covered by the Art Department. They need to read carefully through the script, find props and have them ready and available. The Art Department is also in charge of decorating the set, even if certain items are not specifically called for in the script.

If you need a set built because you're shooting, say, the inside of a space capsule, your creative and fun-loving Art Department will build that "capsule" out of cardboard, aluminum foil and silver paint. But they have to know what you want—and they have to have the time to build it.

4) Costumes/Wardrobe. The Wardrobe person must go through the script with the director and the actors and decide what each of characters is going to wear in each scene. It is critical that wardrobe control the clothes during production. The clothes the male lead wears in the scene inside the drugstore should be the same clothes he wears when he walks out of the drugstore. It may be that those two scenes are shot on different days. What if, in the interim, the actor loses those clothes, or forgets to bring them? He'll be wearing one shirt inside the store. When he walks out of the store, he'll be wearing a different shirt—and the two shots will not match. Maintain the continuity of wardrobe by carefully guarding the wardrobe.

In choosing wardrobe, be aware that red, blaze orange and bright white do not work well on video. Stripes and checks also tend to cause problems on video.

5) Make-up and Hair. This is a fun job for a student who likes to play with make-up and hair. Make-up and Hair, like every other department, requires planning during preproduction. Using the example of the scene in the drugstore, if the hair is styled one way for the interior, it must match on the exterior shot that immediately follows, even though the exterior scene might be shot days later. Make-up and hair must maintain their continuity.

6) Director. Frank Capra said that production is like a caterpillar with hundreds of legs. The director is the head of the caterpillar. As long as the "head" appears to know what it is doing, the legs can do their job. But, if the "head" appears lost, the legs lose direction. On the first day of shooting, everyone on the crew is going to turn to the director and ask, "What do you want?" The director had better know. He will know because of preparation.

The director's job in preproduction is to rehearse the actors, prepare a shot-list, and, possibly, storyboard some of the scenes. (More about storyboard and shot-list in the chapter on directing.)

It's a good idea to rehearse, if possible, in the actual location. Through being in the actual location, one of the actors may discover something he could do that he might not have thought of otherwise. The director may get new ideas about how to shoot the scene, once she sees it being rehearsed in the actual location. It's better to explore the scene with the actors while you have plenty of time. In production you will not have much time to explore.

Once the scene has been explored, it's a good idea to block the scene, deciding where the actors will sit, stand and move within the scene.

Once blocking has been decided upon, the director makes a shot-list. She will start with a master shot (the shot where all the action in the scene takes place), then decide how she wants to cover that scene. (Coverage means the close-ups, medium shots or cutaway shots that will, later, be edited together with the master shot.)

Drawing a "floor plan" of the scene, she will indicate where she wants the camera set-up for each shot. There will be a camera set-up for the master shot and one for each of the medium shots and close-ups. In addition to indicating where the camera will be, the director will decide the order in which she plans to shoot each shot. If you are lighting, say, toward the back of a room, you want to get all the shots in that direction first—before turning around to do the shots toward the front of the room. The fewer times you re-light, the faster the production moves along. For an example of a diagram indicating camera positions, see the chapter on Directing.

Finally, the director can prepare by doing a storyboard—characters drawn in the frame of a movie screen. The storyboard shows the sequence of action, from one shot to the next, within the scene. The storyboard can be helpful in deciding how to shoot a scene. It is easier to decide in preproduction than during production when people are staring at you with that "Do-you-know-what-you're-doing?" look.

A storyboard can also be helpful to the crew. Sometimes, the director is the only one with the shots in his head. This leaves the crew working hard, but not sure where they're heading. If there's a storyboard on the set, showing how one shot leads to the next, it helps the crew see what the director wants. It helps the crew feel more involved. For an illustration of a storyboard, see the chapter on Directing.

While it is enormously valuable to prepare, every director should allow herself the freedom to make changes later. In the process of shooting a scene, there can be creative mistakes, sudden insights and magic moments. The pressure of working on the scene can make something happen that could not have been seen earlier in preproduction. Be prepared. But, at the same time, be open to the creativity of the moment and the magic it might bring.

THE PRODUCTION MEETING

Have your first production meeting as soon as you complete the screenplay. All the members of the crew should be there. Read through the script carefully. Come up with ideas about locations, actors, props and wardrobe. Come up with all kinds of ideas about how to make the movie. You should come out of that meeting knowing who is going to direct, shoot camera, record sound, etc. It's now time to get to work, gathering all the props, and finding the locations and actors you discussed in the meeting.

You may have more meetings along the way. Before you shoot, though, have one final production meeting. This is a chance for everyone (this time crew and cast) to get together and read the script one more time. Sit around a table and read the script slowly, discussing things like props, wardrobe and lighting. It's a great chance for everyone to ask questions and make sure everything that needed to be done has been done.

Once you have prepared all you can prepare, though, it's time to start production. If everything is not perfect, don't worry. Everything will never be perfect. Prepare to the best of your ability, within a reasonable amount of time, then begin. It's going to be fun!

Directing

A movie director is a storyteller. A writer tells stories with words. A director tells stories with images, sound, music and actors. If you want me to tell you how to be a good director, I'm not sure I can do that. But, I can tell you some of the things a good director has to know, like preparation, master shots, coverage, matching action, continuity, cutting on the action, clean entrances and exits, crossing the line, working with actors and more. Knowing these basics will not guarantee you'll be a good director, but they will guarantee you a great start.

The thing the audience cares about the most is the story. So, the most important thing for a director to do is tell a good story. Actually, the director re-tells a story. Has anyone ever told you a joke? And you walked down the hall and re-told the joke? Did you tell it exactly the way it was told to you? No way! You spiced it up with your own style, right? That's what a director does. He re-tells a story, using his own style. To do that, he needs to know how to work with actors and how to choose the "shots" that add up to tell a story.

MASTER SHOT AND COVERAGE

In order to understand some of the rules of directing, let's define the terms "shot," "master shot" and "coverage."

You've all taken a simple photograph. The only difference between a simple photo shot and a movie shot is that, in a movie, the subjects move and the camera moves.

The master shot is any shot that covers all the action of the scene, from the beginning to the end.

The coverage is any shot (medium, close-up, or cutaway) designed to be edited with the master shot.

How and when these shots are used depends entirely upon what shots the director thinks he needs to tell his story. To learn the steps the director takes to choose these shots, let's talk about how the director prepares.

THE DIRECTOR DURING PREPRODUCTION

The first thing the director does is read the script. If it's the director's responsibility to re-tell that story, she had better get a solid understanding of the story. The director has a story conference with the writer, or any member of the crew who wants to offer story input. Once the story is clear, it's time for the production meeting.

THE PRODUCTION MEETING

The director and crew gather around a table and read the script aloud. Read it through several times. Have members of the crew play different characters in the script. Stop and ask questions. How will this shot be done? Is this shot realistic? Will this scene be day or night? What props are called for? If the script calls for a "space ship," what does it look like? What ideas do the kids have about locations and actors? Now is the time to talk about new ideas, and raise any issue. When production starts, it's difficult to make changes. During this meeting (or this series of meetings), decide who will shoot camera, record sound, etc. Once you've talked about all the issues, it's time for the crew to fan out to look for actors, locations, props and equipment. The director should be part of the process in approving actors and locations.

Once the movie is cast and locations secured, the director rehearses with the actors. They should rehearse at least some of the scenes in the actual locations where they plan to shoot. During these rehearsals, the director should be open to input from the actors. Also during rehearsals, the director begins to formulate a shot-list.

THE SHOT-LIST

To make a shot-list, the director closes her eyes and sees the movie in her mind. As she watches the movie on this wonderful internal movie screen, she writes down the shots that she sees, the shots she needs to tell her story.

In order to make a shot-list and ensure that these shots will cut together properly, there are rules every director needs to know. These rules deal with screen direction, matching action, continuity, cutting on the action and clean entrances and exits.

SCREEN DIRECTION

If a character is moving left to right on the screen, that is his "screen direction." If you cut from a wide shot of that character to a closer shot, the character must continue to be moving left to right. If you have a character moving directly toward (or directly away from) the camera, then he is moving neither right nor left on the screen. This means he has a neutral screen direction. When you cut to his coverage, you are free to cut to the character moving left to right, or right to left, whatever best suits the needs of your scene.

MATCHING ACTION

Matching action means that every action must be repeated the same way in the coverage that it was in the master shot.

Imagine a scene with two girls. In the master shot, girl A hands girl B a glass of tea, using her right hand.

When you go in for coverage, girl A must hand girl B the tea, using her right hand. That's called "matching the action." If she hands her the tea with her left hand, when you get in the editing room later, the action won't match.

CONTINUITY

The term "continuity" covers matching the action and screen direction. Continuity also means matching items like props, wardrobe and make-up & hair. Imagine, in the previous example, that girl B is wearing a red baseball cap in the master. When you go in for coverage, girl B must continue to wear that same red cap, or wardrobe continuity from the master to the close-up will not match.

If an actor hands another actor a full glass of tea in the master, when you go in for coverage, that glass of tea must be full. That's matching prop continuity.

Imagine that an actress does a scene, wearing her hair in a pony tail. If she walks out of one shot and, immediately, into another, her hair must continue to be in a pony tail, or make-up & hair continuity will not match.

EYE-LINE CONTINUITY

Imagine a master shot where four people are seated around a table, talking. As they talk, they look at each other the way people do in most normal conversations.

Eye-line means the direction an actor is looking (at a certain point) in the master shot. If we want to cut from the master shot to a close-up on a certain line of dialogue, or at a certain point in the master, we need to match the eye-line in the close-up with the eye-line in the master.

THE SCRIPT SUPERVISOR

In Hollywood, the Script Supervisor is in charge of noting the action that takes place in the master shot — and making sure it stays in continuity in the coverage. This is a great job for one of your crew members. It's a job that will prove to be important later in editing. It's a job that will force a student to learn these all-important rules.

While these rules of continuity are the responsibility of the Script Supervisor (and the camera person), they are rules that every director has to understand in order to make a shot-list.

Man moving left to right in wide shot...

Must continue to move left to right in the following shot.

There are two more rules that are helpful to a director when designing shots—cutting on the action and clean entrances and exits.

CUTTING ON THE ACTION

Cutting on the action is covered in the chapter on editing, but it's important for directing, too. If the director doesn't plan for cutting on the action, the necessary footage may not be there when it's time to edit.

When we edit, we want to create a seamless flow, from one shot to the next. Shots cut together better, without the audience being aware of a cut, if we cut on the action.

Imagine a master shot where a boy walks across the kitchen and sticks his hand into a cookie jar. If you cut from the master shot to the close-up of the cookie jar, just as the boy reaches into the jar, you will be cutting from one shot to the next "on the action." The viewer's eye will tend to follow the action and not notice the cut.

CLEAN ENTRANCES AND EXITS

Let's go back to that cookie jar. We open the scene on the kitchen. The boy enters the kitchen. That's called a "clean entrance." In other words, the boy is not already in the shot when the scene begins. He enters the shot.

Clean entrances give you a cut point you may need later in editing. If you don't need the clean entrance in editing, you don't have to use it. But, if you need it, you'd sure better have shot it while you had the chance.

Likewise, at the end of the scene, it's best to have the boy clear frame with a clean exit. Again, it provides you with a "cut point" if you need it later in editing.

Clean entrances and exits apply to close-ups as well. In the previous scene, the boy walks across the kitchen in the master shot and reaches for the cookie jar. When shooting the close-up of the cookie jar, have the boy's hand enter frame, making a clean entrance.

If you shot the close-up with his hand already in the jar, you'd have a problem. In the editing room, you would be forced to wait for the boy to cross the kitchen in the master shot, then stick his hand into the cookie jar. If you have a clean entrance on the close-up of the cookie jar, you would be free to cut to that close-up earlier.

VARY THE ANGLE

When cutting from one shot to another, it's best to vary the camera angle. For example, if you cut from a medium shot to a close-up, don't shoot the close-up from the same angle you used for the medium shot. Vary the angle.

THE STORYBOARD

The director sees the movie in his mind and imagines each shot. The storyboard is a series of drawings, showing how those shots fit together in the scene. It's easier to think about things like screen direction and match action when you're alone than when ten people are staring at you, wondering what you're going to do next.

You don't have to be Picasso to draw a storyboard. Draw stick figures. Pay particular attention to which way the nose is pointing. (Left to right, or right to left). You'll see, later, how noses help you maintain screen direction.

This storyboard example tells us that:

1) The male character waves in a wide shot, looking left to right.

2) The male character continues to wave in a close-up, still looking left to right.

3) The female character waves in a wide shot, looking right to left. The arrow indicates that she exits frame, moving right to left.

4) The two meet in a wide shot, with the female character entering frame, moving right to left.

You don't need to storyboard every shot in the movie—just the complicated scenes, where the storyboard will help.

SHOT DIAGRAM

A "bird's eye view" of how the director plans to cover the scene, complete with camera positions, can also be helpful. The diagram below shows where the director plans to place her camera for the master shot and for two medium shots. The numbers next to each shot indicate the order in which she plans to shoot each shot. The master shot (M) is first. A medium shot (MS) is second. Another medium shot is third. A cutaway shot (CW) of the doorway is fourth.

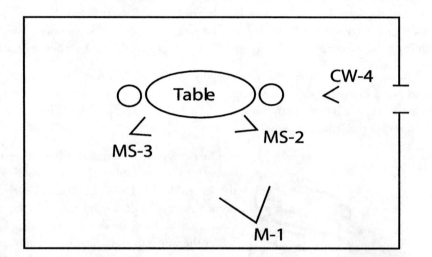

Alfred Hitchcock did storyboards for every shot in his movie. Other directors avoid too much preparation, leaving the door open for inspiration. While the director should always be open to new ideas, she must also prepare.

The director must have a plan when she walks on the set. She can change the plan later, but she must start with a plan. She formulates that plan beginning with:

a) A shot-list.

b) Some scenes storyboarded.

c) Some scenes diagrammed.

The shot-list must cover the scene with a realistic number of camera set-ups. Too much coverage is not necessary and can take so much time that you get behind in production.

Notice how much of a director's time is in the planning process. Remember what Frank Capra said, "The key to a good production is good preproduction."

Finally, the first day of production arrives. The director won't feel ready (no director ever feels ready), but it's time to start anyway.

THE FIRST DAY ON THE SET

The crew arrives on location with equipment, props and wardrobe. The actors arrive, prepared and eager.

The director walks on the set. The crew looks at the director. Finally, the camera person utters those words guaranteed to terrify any director on the first day of shooting: "Where do you want the camera?"

The director knows the answer because he's prepared. The first thing he does before designating the first camera set-up, though, is to rehearse the scene. Even if he's already rehearsed the scene in this location, he rehearses again. Rehearsal lets the crew see what the director is trying to achieve. It gives the camera person, the sound person and the lighting person the opportunity to see where the actors will move within the scene.

The actors rehearse the scene from beginning to end. It is not important that the actors give a dramatic performance during this rehearsal. It's more important that they make sure they know where to move and how to handle props. They should save their emotions for the "take."

Once everyone understands where the actors will move, the director explains how she plans to "cover" the scene. How and why the director covers the scene the way she does is entirely up to her own artistic sensibilities. By showing how she plans to cover the scene, though, the director allows the members of the crew to feel more included. When they go to work hanging lights, they will know what they're working toward. Also, talking about coverage gives cast and crew one last chance to catch problems or offer creative input.

Once everyone has seen the master shot and the coverage, the director and the actors leave the set and the crew begins to light. The camera person should give the director some idea of when they will be ready to shoot. Knowing how much time they have, the director and actors continue to rehearse, or the actors get into make-up and wardrobe.

When the crew is ready, the director and actors return to the set. The lights are ready. The camera is ready.

The director walks the actors through the scene one more time, with the camera person watching. Lights may have to be adjusted. Cables may have to be hidden. Once this is done, you're ready for the first "take."

The director gets everybody into position, calls for "quiet," tells camera to "roll," then, when she's ready, calls "action." The actors play through the scene, just like a scene in a play. When it's over, the director calls "cut."

Did the scene work for the director? If so, was everything okay for "camera"? How do the actors feel about the scene? Is there something they think they can do better?

If the director feels she can do the scene better, she makes adjustments with the actors and/or the camera person—and they go to "take 2." The time-consuming thing about making movies is getting the equipment, lights, etc., into position. The time it takes to do another "take" does not matter at all. And the small cost of the videotape for another "take" certainly does not matter. The director should keep doing "takes" until she feels the master shot is as good as she can get it. Not perfect. Just as good as she can get it, within a reasonable period of time.

Once the master is done, it's time to do the coverage.

WHAT'S THE CORRECT WAY TO "COVER" THE MASTER?

There is no "correct" way. The shots the director chooses are the shots that he thinks best tell the story.

The old system in Hollywood required that a scene open with the master shot. After the master, they would cut to an over-the-shoulder shot, then a medium shot, then a close-up. This formula grew out of the studio system where the editing department had nothing to do with the production. The editing department simply received reels of film every day. They were supposed to edit that film in accordance with the script. The directors in the studio system were required to cover their scenes in that formulaic way to ensure that the editing department would have the necessary coverage to complete the film. It was "assembly line" editing.

But you don't have to make movies by a formula. When deciding how to cover a scene, see the scene in your mind. What shot do you see coming up next? Use that shot.

Remember the lessons we have covered. Action must match. Continuity must be maintained with props, wardrobe, screen direction. Eye-lines must match. When you do your coverage, try to use clean entrances and exits. And plan shots so that, later, you'll be able to cut on the action.

But even these rules can be broken if it helps you tell your story. Choose your shots based on what you need to tell your story. If your action doesn't match, nobody will care—as long as they care about your story.

When doing coverage, shoot the coverage shot from the beginning of the scene to the end. Imagine you shot a master of four people seated at a table, talking. Now, you're doing a close-up of one of those people. Shoot the close-up, from the beginning of the scene to the end of the scene. In the close-up, the character delivers his lines—just like he did in the master. While you're on his close-up, get footage of that same actor listening and reacting to the others at the table—just like he did in the master. You'll find that covering each close-up, medium shot, etc. from the beginning of the scene to the end will provide you with more options later in editing.

IT'S A GOOD IDEA TO SHOOT THE MASTER FIRST

If you shoot the master shot first, then—when it comes time to do all the close-ups and medium shots—you will already know the proper screen direction for everything in the scene. Because you know a certain character reaches for a drink with his right hand in the master, you will be able to easily match that action later in the close-up. Shooting the master first provides a road map, of sorts, that helps guide us in how to match the coverage.

Every master does not have to be covered. It's very possible that a well-designed master shot will work all by itself. It's still a good idea to shoot at least one cutaway.

THE CUTAWAY SHOT

A cutaway is a shot separate from what the viewer sees in the master shot. If the master is four people seated at a table, a cutaway shot might be the clock on the nearby wall. We have to "cut away" from the master to see the clock.

The cutaway could include the actors in the master, but it would have to be a part of the actor that we don't see in the master shot, like a foot tapping or a hand twirling a key ring under the table, so that, if necessary, we could "cut away" to that shot and it would take us, momentarily, away from the master shot.

An effective cutaway shot can be extremely valuable. If we have, say, a master shot that plays thirty seconds and we want to cut it down to fifteen seconds, going to a cutaway shot, then back to the master, could give us the option to do that. If we didn't have the cutaway, there would be no way to get away from the master and shorten the scene. The cutaway should be, somehow, connected with the story, so it doesn't look like you're going to a cutaway for no good reason. It's important to get a cutaway shot with every scene, in case you "cross the line."

CROSSING THE LINE

Most movie makers goof up screen direction by violating a rule called "crossing the line."

Imagine a scene where two characters are talking. Character A faces left to right. Character B faces right to left. Imagine a line, running from one nose to the other.

The two actors play out the scene in the master shot. When the director decides the master shot is good enough, she goes in for coverage.

For story reasons, let's say, the director wants a medium shot of actor A, with a road sign in the background. Because of where the road sign is located, the director crosses the imaginary line to get the medium shot of character A—with the road sign behind him.

Later, in editing, the director discovers that, in the master shot, Character A is facing left to right. But now, when she cuts to the medium shot, suddenly Character A is facing right to left. By crossing the line, the director caused Character A's screen direction to suddenly change directions. This abrupt change in screen direction, for no apparent reason, will confuse the audience.

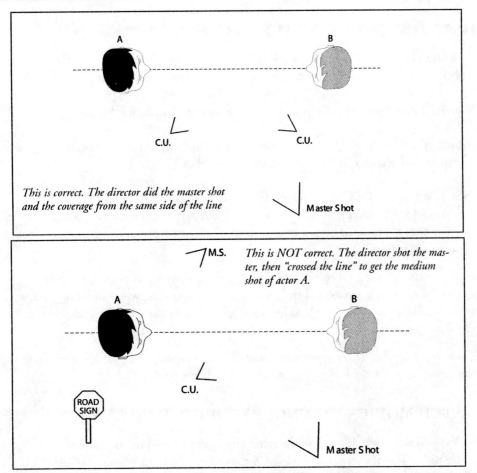

This is correct. The director did the master shot and the coverage from the same side of the line

This is NOT correct. The director shot the master, then "crossed the line" to get the medium shot of actor A.

If the director had shot the coverage from the same side of the imaginary line where she'd shot the master, the screen direction on Character A would have remained the same.

There is a simple way to avoid crossing the line. When you shoot your master shot, notice the direction each character's nose is pointing. Is it pointing left to right? Or right to left? When you go in for coverage, simply keep that character's nose pointed in the same screen direction.

IF THE AUDIENCE SEES THE CHANGE IN SCREEN DIRECTION TAKE PLACE, THEY WILL ACCEPT IT.

Let's go back to the shot where Character A is looking left to right and Character B is looking right to left.

Imagine that, this time, we are doing a dolly shot. While the characters play out the scene, the camera dollies around the actors, coming to rest on a medium shot of character A, with the road sign in the background. At this point character A is looking right to left. His screen direction has changed, but the audience saw it happen, so it doesn't matter! They accept it.

HOW THE CUTAWAY SHOT CAN SAVE YOU

The audience tends to forget screen direction quickly which gives you, the movie maker, the opportunity to fix a screen direction problem in editing. It works like this:

Shot 1: The audience sees Character A in the master shot, facing left to right.

Shot 2: A car drives up. (Cutaway shot of the car arriving. In this shot, we don't see either of the actors that we saw in the master shot.)

Shot 3: We cut back to Character A. This time he is facing right to left. Character A changed screen direction, but the audience did not tend to notice—because the cutaway shot of the car arriving caused the audience to forget Character A's previous screen direction.

If you change screen directions by crossing the line, you can often get out of trouble by going to a cutaway shot. That's why it's important, when shooting a scene, to shoot at least one cutaway shot. Even though you may not need it, it could save you later in editing.

Be aware of what "crossing the line" means and try to avoid it. If you can't avoid it, though, keep going. If your story is engaging enough, the audience won't care.

WATCH MOVIES TO UNDERSCORE THESE LESSONS

You will never watch a movie the same way again. One of the benefits of being a movie maker is that every time you watch a movie you can learn from the best.

Get your students together, grab a video of *ET*, and review these lessons, learning from Mr. Spielberg.

Watching *ET*:

1) Find examples of matching action.

2) Find examples of screen direction matching from the master shot to the coverage.

3) Find examples of screen direction matching from shot to shot.

4) Find a place where screen direction changes in the scene. (For example, a character walking left to right turns and walks right to left.)

5) Find a place where the camera moves, causing an actor's screen direction to change, but the audience sees the change take place.

6) Find examples of prop continuity.

7) Find examples of wardrobe continuity.

8) Find examples of make-up & hair continuity.

9) Notice where Spielberg cuts on the action.

10) Find examples of clean entrances. (You may not see the clean entrance, but if the edit is made just as a character, or object, enters frame, that's a clean entrance.)

11) Find examples of clean exits.

12) Count the number of camera set-ups Spielberg used to shoot a scene. (A camera set-up is each time the camera is positioned for a shot in a particular scene. If a director shot a scene using one master shot and two close-ups, that would be three camera set-ups for that scene.) Watch where Spielberg places the camera and count the number of set-ups. Don't count the number of shots. Count the number of camera set-ups.

13) Can you find a situation where Spielberg crossed the line? Can you find a situation where a cutaway shot may have saved Spielberg from abruptly changing screen direction?

14) Notice how Spielberg varies the camera angle when he goes from one shot to the next.

15) Notice that if a master shot fulfills the purpose of the scene, you don't have to cover that master shot.

16) Notice that, when Spielberg goes in for coverage, there is no formula. He weaves the magic of his shots, depending upon the shots he needs to re-tell the story.

WORKING WITH ACTORS

You may be able to work with experienced actors. You may not. It doesn't matter. The actors you find for your production will be perfect, just the way they are.

You know more than you think you know. If you used your common sense in casting, you should be okay. Once you have the actors cast, though, how does a director work with them?

First of all, you want the actor to understand his character's purpose in the scene. What does the character want? Why is he there? The actor needs to understand the given circumstances that surround the scene.

If the character enters the scene to get a cookie because he is hungry, that's one set of circumstances. If the character enters the scene to steal the cookie because his mother told him he could not have one, that's a different set of circumstances. If the character enters the kitchen to steal the cookie—because his mother said he could not have one—and his mother is asleep in a chair across the room, that's yet another set of circumstances. The lines may be the same, but the given circumstances can alter the way the actor says the lines.

NO ACTING, PLEASE!

When some hear the word "act," they think it means to be bigger than life—talk louder than normal—make bigger gestures. That's the way people act in the school play, but that's not the way they should perform in a movie.

There is no need to "enunciate" to the back of the room or emote with broad gestures. The best film acting should not be obvious. You want actors to look like they're not acting. There is no simple explanation for how to act. But I can offers suggestions for how to deal with actors and how to keep them from trying to over-act.

First of all, actors feel vulnerable. Everybody is responsible for making the movie, but the actor is the one whom the audience will see. Some actors will feel insecure or fear that they will look silly or stupid.

Build confidence in your actors. Tell them that what they're doing is great. I'm not suggesting you give them false praise. When you want something about a performance changed, say, "That was great, but this time could you try it like this. . . ." It gets you the change you want, without taking away the confidence they need.

The actors' purpose is not to simply say the lines. Their job is to deliver the lines honestly, within the given circumstances of the scene. Let's go back to the scene where the boy enters the kitchen to get a cookie. Imagine, now, that the mother enters the kitchen and catches the boy. We know, from an earlier scene, that the mother told him to not get another cookie. Now, though, the mother enters, sees the boy and asks, "Are you taking a cookie?" The boy looks at her, the life behind his eyes desperately saying that he is trying to figure a way out of this. Finally, in a pitiful lie, he says, "No."

Do you see how different the scene would have been if the boy had simply and quickly said, "No"? We would have lost the life behind the words. Good acting gives us the life behind the words.

There is an acting exercise called "the magic if" where the actor tries to imagine how he would feel if he were in the same situation as the character. Have the actor, literally, ask himself, what would he do if he were in that same situation? How would he feel in that situation?

For most, though, let acting simply be "play acting." Let it be a fun game of make believe where they "play like" they're this character or that character. They've been playing make believe, or pretend, since they were three years old. Acting is pretend. Just ask them to pretend, within the given circumstances of the scene.

WORKING WITH CHILDREN

You will, at times, find yourself working with children who are too young to take direction. That's fine. Hollywood deals with this all the time. You can use the same method Hollywood uses to get a good performance: trickery.

I'm not suggesting that you tell a child a lie. There are the old Hollywood stories of Shirley Temple being told that her puppy had died, so they could get her to cry in the scene. I don't want anything like that, and I know you don't either. I'm talking about trickery that is harmless.

In *Close Encounters of the Third Kind*, there was the little boy who opened the door to see the "light." As he opened the door, the boy looked out and marveled at the magic of what he saw. Spielberg could hardly have asked the little boy for a performance. He was much too young. Spielberg solved the problem with a clown. Without ever letting the little boy know that there was a clown on the other side of the door, Spielberg positioned his cameras then told the boy to open the door. As the cameras rolled, the boy opened the door and looked out. What he saw was a clown, doing wonderful "clown" things. His little face reacted to what he saw. When Spielberg edited the scene there was, of course, no clown. It looked like the boy was reacting to the "light" from "the close encounter."

As a director, you have license to do whatever you want, as long as it is safe and doesn't hurt anybody's feelings, to get the reaction you want from your actor.

REHEARSING ON LOCATION

When rehearsing the actors at the actual location, give the actors "marks," places on the floor, or ground, where you want the actor to stop, turn, or move in another direction.

"Marks" are critical. If an actor walks across the floor and stops wherever he wants to stop, he might block the camera's view of another actor, or he might walk out of frame. To avoid that, the director will want the actor to stop in a certain place, or "hit his mark."

When rehearsing before the shoot, the director and camera person will give the actor "marks," designated with a small piece of black tape. (The camera is less likely to see black tape.) One of the challenges of acting in movies is hitting "marks" without looking down to find them. Unless there is some motivation to be looking down, don't let the actor look down to find his "mark."

LET'S TRY A "TAKE"

By this point, you have rehearsed your master shot. The actors know their lines. They have their "marks" and know where to look (eye-lines). The camera and lights are ready.

The director will ask the sound person if she is ready. Ask camera if he is ready. Once camera gets a slate (scene and "take" number) the director calls for quiet, then tells camera to "roll."

Once camera is rolling, the director calls "action." The actors start the scene, just like they rehearsed it.

If a member of the cast or crew makes a mistake, stop. Don't blame anybody. Keep an upbeat attitude. Patiently solve the problem. Build confidence in the actors. Thumbs up to the crew. Then go for another take.

The three most important words in movie making are "com," "pro," "mise." Do the best you can, smile and keep going. This is supposed to be fun.

THE SILLY EXERCISE

If your actors are insecure because they think they're going to look silly, try the "silly exercise." In the silly exercise each actor and member of the crew has to do everything they can to look silly—contort faces, lie down on the floor, roll, do weird things with their eyes and tongue. If everybody on the set is willing to look silly, it takes away the actors' fears. If you feel the actors are not opening up, shout, "Silly exercise!" The rule is everybody (director included) has to jump right into the silly exercise. It works like magic to open up your actors, take away their fears, and lighten up the set.

THE BEST RULE OF THUMB ABOUT ACTING

Have fun with it. Try it one way. If that doesn't work, try it another way. If the actor feels uncomfortable saying the lines as written, be open to changing the lines, the blocking, or both.

Do all you can to build confidence in your actors. Never tell them they're not good. You may have made some unwise choices in casting, but—right now—the actors are doing the best they can. If they can't do the scene one way, try it another way, but keep building their confidence.

Let the actors offer creative input, but don't let them take charge. The director is in charge. If there's more than one boss on the set, it can lead to chaos. Chaos can lead to frustration. Frustration can cause people to quit. The only way to fail is to quit.

Let's review:

1) Get a good understanding of the story—and of how you plan to tell the story.

2) Cast to the best of your ability.

3) Close your eyes and see the movie in your mind. Make a shot-list of what you see. Work to make that list realistic for the production time that you have.

4) Storyboard and/or diagram some of the scenes.

5) Rehearse the actors. Help them understand the given circumstances of each scene and their goal in each scene. Rehearse in the actual location, if possible.

6) Have one final production meeting with every member of cast and crew present. Go through the script, with each actor reading his or her part. Make sure the cast and crew understand the needs of each scene and accept responsibility for their particular job in each scene. Are there any last-minute questions about props, wardrobe or who is doing what job? Now is the time to make sure every detail is handled.

7) First day of shooting: Walk the actors through the scene. Make sure they know where to sit, stand and move. Give them "marks." Make sure Sound, Camera and Lighting know where the actors will sit, stand and move in the scene.

8) Direct the scene. Believe in yourself. You know more than you think you know.

9) When directing the actors, build their confidence. Be supportive and upbeat to the crew.

And, remember, if you can direct one scene, you can direct a whole movie. A movie is nothing more than a bunch of scenes strung together, with a through-line, the spine of the story, the thread that holds it all together.

And also remember the most important thing of all—have fun!

NOTES:

Camera

The camcorder consists of two basic parts, the lens and the body. (Audio is part of the camcorder too, but—in this chapter—we're dealing with picture only.) The purpose of the lens is to focus light in such a way as to cause an image, or picture, to be recorded onto the video tape. The purpose of the body is to hold the videotape and move it forward at the steady rate of thirty frames per second while images are recorded to the tape. The purpose of the camera is to record shots that add up to make a movie.

To get those shots, we're going to cover:

1) Exposure

2) Color temperature

3) Focus

4) Depth of field

5) Lenses (wide, normal, telephoto)

6) Composition

7) Camera moves

8) Color

EXPOSURE

Exposure means the amount of light that comes through the lens in order to create a picture on video. If it's dark where you're shooting, a small amount of light will come through the lens. If it's bright, more light will come through. You want to control how much light comes through the lens so your picture will be exposed properly. The aperture is a mechanism in the camera that opens and closes, controlling the amount of light that comes through the lens.

Most camcorders have automatic exposure. The electronic "eye" in the camera reads the light being reflected back into the lens—and the camera automatically opens or closes the aperture, depending upon the amount of light the picture needs for what most viewers consider to be a normal exposure.

Automatic exposure can present problems. If you have a character in the shade in the left side of the frame—and another character in the sun on the right side of the frame, automatic exposure will "average" the shade and the sunlight and expose for something in between. You may not want that.

If automatic exposure presents a problem, check your manual to see if you can override automatic exposure and set the exposure on your camcorder manually. If not, solve the problem creatively by re-staging the scene—putting all of the actors either in the shade, or in the sunlight.

COLOR TEMPERATURE AND "WHITE BALANCE"

White balance adjusts the camcorder for the different colors of light. Humans don't see the different colors of light because the eye is so good at adjusting, but the camcorder sees them. Sunlight has a blue tint. The light from a reading lamp has a reddish, orange glow. Light from fluorescent bulbs casts a greenish color. We adjust for these different colors of light when we white balance.

Most camcorders have automatic white balance. For those that don't, though, white balancing is a simple process. Place a white card (a sheet of white typing paper will do) in the light you're using for your scene. Point the camcorder at the white paper so it sees nothing but "white," then push the "white balance" button. The camera will adjust to the color of the light reflecting from the white paper.

Whenever you move to a new location, redo the "white balance" on your camcorder. If you moved from outside (the blue of sunlight) to inside (the orange of tungsten), you would need to do another "white balance."

FOCUS

You know what focus means—the picture is "sharp," not "fuzzy." Most camcorders have automatic focus. Again, that means that an electric "eye" automatically focuses on an object in the frame. That's fine as long as it's focusing on what you want. If it's not, you have a problem.

Imagine you have a character fairly close to the camera and, for artistic reasons, you have placed that character in the right side of the frame. The "electronic eye" focuses on an object in the center of the frame. If the object in the center of the frame is in the distance, then the object in the distance will be in focus, but the character you've placed in the right side of the frame will not be in focus.

The two ways to correct this problem are—to override automatic focus and focus the camera manually; or re-stage the scene so that what you want to be in focus will be in the area of the "electronic focusing eye."

GETTING A SHARP FOCUS

If you can set focus manually, here's a way to ensure sharp focus. Compose your shot the way you want it, then zoom all the way in on the most distant actor in your shot that you want to be in focus. Zoom in on an area that has detail, like eyes. Adjust your focus knob until the eyelashes are sharp. Then, zoom back, widening your lens until you have the same shot that you composed originally. This way, everything from that distant actor back to within a few feet in front of the camera will be in focus.

PULLING FOCUS (FOLLOW FOCUS)

If you have a shot where the actor moves from a point thirty feet away from the camera to a point five feet from the camera, that actor may not be in focus during the entire shot. If not, you will need to "follow" focus.

If your camcorder will allow you to focus manually, there will be a focus knob or ring. Indicate where the focus knob needs to be for the beginning of the shot (when the actor is thirty feet away) and for the end of the shot (when the actor is five feet away). When the actor begins to move toward camera, have the assistant camera person "follow focus" by adjusting the focus knob (or ring) as the actor moves closer. This keeps the actor in focus throughout the shot.

If you cannot override automatic focus, you can follow focus automatically. Again, though, you can run into the problem of what the camera, not you, thinks should be in focus. If the camera focuses on the actor as he moves closer, then you have no problem. But, if the electronic eye "sees" the actor, then "sees" the distant back wall, it will focus first for the actor, then for the wall, then back to the actor. This is called "searching focus," and it can be annoying. Try re-staging the scene so the "electronic eye" stays on the actor the whole time—and does not "search."

DEPTH OF FIELD

"Depth of field" means the point in front of your actor to a point behind your actor where everything is in focus. Depth of field is, literally, the "field," the area, in front of your camcorder where everything is in focus.

The way the new camcorders are built, you probably won't have a problem with depth of field. But, again, you need to understand the concept. If you have a problem with depth of field (and it's certainly possible), then this lesson will teach you how to increase your depth of field.

Imagine you're shooting a scene where three children are seated at a kitchen table. The table is in the foreground of the shot. One of the children gets up from the table and walks into the background. Twenty feet from the camera, the child turns and delivers a line. The children still seated at the table, in the foreground, are five feet from the camera. For all three characters to remain in focus, the "depth of field" will have to at least be from five feet in front of the camera to twenty feet in front of the camera.

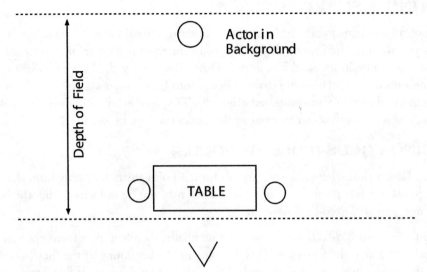

Every character does not have to be in focus. You may want a character in the background to go "fuzzy." That's an artistic decision. But, if you want certain characters to be in focus, they must remain within your depth of field.

Or, you have to increase your depth of field.

1) You can increase your depth of field, by widening your lens. If, in the example above, the boy in the background goes out of focus before delivering his line, zoom out and widen the lens. (The wider the lens, the greater the depth of field.)

2) You can increase your depth of field by closing down your aperture. Remember aperture? Open it up to let in more light. Close it down to let in less light. The more you close the aperture, the more you increase your depth of field. It's like squinting. More things are in focus when you squint. In order to close down the aperture, though, we have to add light. We could either add more lights, or—if we don't have more lights—become a creative problem solver. One way to creatively solve our problem (in this scene with the children at the table) would be move the scene to an exterior porch of the house. Suddenly, we have more light from the sun. The aperture will close down and the depth of field will increase.

3) Your depth of field increases as your actors get further from the camera. This simply means that, the further you put all of the actors from the camera, the more likely it is that they will be in focus.

Review: Three ways to increase depth of field are:

1) Widen the lens.

2) Close down the aperture by adding light.

3) Move all the actors further away from the camera.

LENSES, FOCAL LENGTH

There are three basic focal lengths of lenses—wide, normal, or "medium," and the telephoto, or "long" lens.

Every camcorder has a zoom lens. By zooming in or out, you will be able to create the focal length of the lens that best suits the needs of your shot. Zooming "in" lengthens the lens. Zooming "out" widens the lens.

If you're doing a master shot of a family gathered around a kitchen table, you may have to use a wide lens to get everybody in the shot, especially if you're blocked by the wall and cannot move back further.

If you want to get a close-up of a person sitting in a boat, you may want to zoom in to a "long" lens.

Every camera has a "normal" lens. Stand behind the camera and look at your actor. Now view the actor through the lens. If the actor looks about the same size, you're looking through the "normal" lens. About 90% of the shots in Hollywood are done through a "normal" lens. The "normal" lens makes things look more, well, normal.

THE WIDE ANGLE LENS

1) Allows you to shoot in areas where you might not be able to shoot otherwise, like a small room, or inside a car.

2) Provides you with greater depth of field.

3) Makes camera bobbles less noticeable. If you do a hand-held shot, the wider the angle, the less the likelihood that the audience will notice a shaky shot.

4) With the angle extremely wide (when using an extra-wide adapter), the picture can distort, or bend at the edges.

5) Can make movements away from the camera or toward the camera appear to be faster than they normally look.

6) Can make actors appear to be further away than they really are. If you're looking through a wide lens and the actor seems too far away, it's because of the wide angle lens.

NORMAL, OR "MEDIUM" LENS

The best lens to use, if it can give you the shot that you want, is the normal lens.

THE TELEPHOTO LENS

Have you ever looked through a pair of binoculars? The telephoto lens is binoculars on a camcorder.

1) The telephoto lens can get you the shot you need, even if you can't get close enough with the camera.

2) The longer the lens, the less the depth of field. Imagine you are shooting a scene that takes place in the wilderness. At the location where you're shooting, there is a gas station behind your actor. You can't move the camera or the actor. Knowing that a telephoto lens decreases depth of field, you could shoot the actor through a long lens in such a way that keeps your actor in focus, but throws the background out of focus. The background will be a blur, but that's better than the background being a gas station.

3) When you shoot through a long lens, camera boggles are more noticeable. If you shoot through a long lens, try to use a tripod—unless you want the shot to look shaky.

THE COMMON LANGUAGE OF SHOTS

Making movies is a collaborative effort. Members of the crew need a common language to describe shots and composition. The language most often used is:

wide shot

over-the-shoulder shot

medium shot

medium shot with holsters

close-up   *extreme close-up*

Medium shot with holsters is a term coined during the days of the B cowboy movies. It meant, literally, a medium shot, wide enough to see the cowboy's holsters. If you want a shot a little wider than a medium shot, call it a "medium shot with holsters." It's all part of the fun.

The diagrams suggest how these shots might be framed. There is no "correct" medium shot or close-up, so don't think you have to copy these examples precisely.

THE STATIC SHOT

The static shot simply means a shot where the camera does not move. The static shot, like the normal lens, is the most commonly used shot in Hollywood. But that doesn't mean you have to use it all the time. This is movies! Come on! Let's move—with the camera that is. Most camera moves have, in the past, required expensive Hollywood equipment. But not anymore. This book and video will show you how you can make any camera move that Hollywood can make.

THE PAN SHOT

With the camera on a tripod, or with the camera hand-held, a pan shot swivels the camera from side to side, from left to right, or right to left. The shot got its name from the camera moving across the countryside, photographing the "panorama," thus the name "pan shot."

1) Have a motivation to pan. A boy rides up on his bicycle. Pan with the boy as he arrives. Your motivation, or reason, for the pan shot is to show the boy arriving.

2) Don't pan too fast. If you pan too fast, the picture can blur.

3) Position yourself for the end of the pan. Imagine you are doing a pan shot of a passing car. The car approaches. You pan with it. The car passes. You need to continue panning, but your body can't twist any further. You try to continue, but you trip, boggle the camera and ruin the end of the shot.

Here's how to do that pan shot successfully. Frame the pan shot where you want it to end. Position your feet for the ending of the shot. Now move back and compose the beginning of the shot. Roll camera. The car enters frame. Pan with the car. This time, when you twist with the pan, your body is already in position for the end of the pan shot.

4) Begin and end your pan shot with a static shot. It can confuse the audience to cut from a static shot to a moving shot, or from a moving shot to a static shot.

Using the example of the boy arriving on his bike: compose the beginning of the shot. Roll camera. Shoot, say, three seconds of footage, then cue the bike to enter. This gives you a static shot at the beginning of the pan. After the bike rides out of frame, hold a beat on the ending static shot before cutting camera.

It can disorient the audience to cut from a static shot straight to a moving pan shot. That's why it's a good idea to have a static shot at the beginning or the end of a pan. It's there, in editing, if you need it.

THE TILT SHOT

A tilt shot is when the camera pivots up or down. If a pan pivots side to side, a tilt pivots up or down. A tilt, like any other shot, needs a motivation. Imagine that a kid turns a corner and finds himself face to face with a pair of shoes. He slowly looks up to see an angry face. The purpose of the tilt is to reveal the angry face.

THE ZOOM

There may be a gene, still active during the teenage years, that causes the young movie maker to zoom in and out a lot with the camcorder. It's called zoomitis, and it's not always the best way to do a shot. A zoom shot, if used, must be motivated, like a pan shot. A zoom shot can be a way of pointing something out. A boy walks into a room, looking for a key. When he sees the key, the director might choose to zoom in on the key, as if to say, "There it is." The best use of the zoom, though, is to allow you to compose your shot easily. Another reason, as mentioned, is to zoom in, find focus, then zoom back out and recompose your shot.

THE DOLLY SHOT

Imagine you're at the movies, staring up at the screen, where you see two actors walking along, talking. You're moving with them as they walk and talk. Something must be moving the camera. Something is. It's called a dolly.

In Hollywood, a dolly is an expensive piece of equipment that holds the camera and rolls. In our program, anything that rolls the camera and is safe can be a "dolly." How many ways can you think of to hold the camera and roll?

1) A wheelchair. Seat your camera person in a wheelchair. Put a bean bag chair in her lap. She can steady the camcorder on top of the bean bag chair. Have a crew member pull her along.

2) Grocery cart. Politely ask your local grocer if you might borrow a grocery cart. It

gets your camera person up higher and would give her more opportunity to shoot off the side of the dolly. Again, she would brace the camera with pillows and/or bean bags—anything that works.

3) A child's wagon makes the perfect height dolly for tracking (dollying) in front of children.

4) A camcorder could be taped to a skateboard while the skateboard is pushed through the house. That could make a nice point-of-view shot of a dog running through the house. How about a small camcorder taped to a remote control car? Dolly shots are limited only by imagination.

Some of the new camcorders have a built-in stabilizer. This stabilizer causes the picture to remain steady while you bump along, getting your dolly shot. There is no way a dolly shot, hand-held from a grocery cart, is going to be perfectly smooth. But, with today's modern camcorders and this new stabilizing device, it's a miracle how smooth your dolly shot can actually be. Check your manual to see if your camcorder has a stabilizer. If so, there's no learning curve to it. Just turn it on. This stabilizer, together with any set of wheels you can dream up, will provide you with an amazing ability to get dolly shots just like Hollywood.

Hollywood also has an expensive device called a "Steadicam." It allows the camera person to, literally, carry the camera while maintaining a smooth shot. The stabilizers in some of the new camcorders can act as a "Steadicam." If the ground is too bumpy to roll, try carrying the camera, with the stabilizer on. You'll be amazed at how steady your hand-held shot can be.

If your camera doesn't have a stabilizer, let your camera move anyway. If you want to, say, follow two actors across a pasture, walk with the camera. Try to hold it as steady as possible. And, remember, the wider the lens, the less shaky the shot. Other than that, though, don't worry about it. Your goal is to tell a story. If the audience cares about your story, they won't care about a shaky shot.

THE BOOM SHOT

A tilt pivots the camera. A boom is when the whole camera is raised or lowered.

You've seen boom shots. The camera is tight on the man on the ground. We hear the sound of police sirens. The CAMERA BOOMS UP, revealing police cars as they arrive.

Or, in another shot, the camera is high, looking across a pasture. We hear the sound of a country tune. The CAMERA BOOMS DOWN to discover a pickup arriving, radio blaring.

1) How about a seesaw? Have your camera person sit on one end of the seesaw, holding the camcorder. Have a crew member stand on each side of the camera person, for

safety. Have the other members of the crew boom the camera person up or down.

Note: this could be dangerous. Please try this exercise with adult supervision.

2) A camera person squatting, then slowly moving up (or down) while holding the camera, would be a boom shot.

3) Tape the camcorder securely to the end of a long board. Lay the board across any fulcrum and boom up or down.

To monitor the shot, run a cable from the camcorder back to a small television on the ground. The director can monitor the shot while the crew booms the camera.

Whatever your mind can conceive, you can achieve—especially with today's modern video technology.

BACKGROUND

When composing a shot, think about what the background "says." If a scene takes place at a county fair, compose the shot so that the background, not the dialogue, tells the audience they're at the fair.

Aunt Myrtle can, somehow, find the ugliest wall in the house to use as a background for photographs. But you can do better. Providing your characters with depth in the background (distance behind the actor), can often help make a more interesting shot.

Beware of things in the background that you do not want in the shot, like a church steeple growing out of your actor's head. What if you're shooting a movie that takes place in the 1920s and there's an air conditioner sticking out of a window in the background? Develop trained eyes that can "see" background advantages and disadvantages.

FOREGROUND

It makes nice composition to frame your actors with something in the foreground, like the limb of a tree, a doorway, an arch or the columns on a porch.

But what if there's no tree around? Make one. Chop a branch off a tree (with per-

mission, of course), carry it to your shot and have crew members hold the branch, framing the shot the same as if there were a tree there, just off camera.

COLOR

Red and blaze orange tend to "bleed" or smear on video. When thinking of wardrobe, try to avoid saturated colors like bright red, blaze orange or bright white. Also, try to avoid stripes and checks.

SLATES, NUMBERING SCENES AND TAKES

When shooting, identify each shot with a "slate." If you get into the editing room later, and you're not able to identify which shot is which, you could find yourself in a confusing and time-consuming mess.

Let's say you're shooting scene 7 from your screenplay. When you shoot the master, slate it 7-1. That means Scene 7, Take 1. Change the "take" number each time you do an added "take."

When you go in for coverage, slate your shots 7A-1 (Scene 7A, take 1), 7B-1 (Scene 7B, take 1), etc. You will see later, in the chapter on editing, how this will help you arrange your shots in an organized manner. Use a small dry-erase board, or chalkboard, to slate your shot. Clap-sticks are used in film production to synchronize the film with the dialogue. Clap-sticks are not necessary in video, since the dialogue is recording right onto the videotape.

PEOPLE MAKE THE PICTURE

In deciding how to compose a shot, it has always helped me to remind myself that "people make the picture." You know how it is when you get together with your family on Thanksgiving and your Aunt Myrtle takes the pictures—and they come back 70% wall and 30% people? Nobody wants to see the wall. People want to see the people. They want to see the "life" of the people come through in the eyes and faces. Compose your shot in any way you want, but remember—you're telling a story about people. The audience will be more interested in the story if they can see people.

LET THE CAMERA MOVE!

This is movies, so let the camcorder move. Don't make the camcorder stay locked to a tripod for the sake of being "correct." It can make your movie lifeless. Let your camera live. If that means having a shaky shot every now and then, so what? You will learn more, given the freedom to move the camera, than you will trying to be "correct" on a tripod. If you want to do the master shot hand-held, then hurry in for coverage, also hand-held, go ahead! The production will move along faster, and—as long as the story is engaging—the audience won't care about a slightly shaky camera. Use the tripod, but feel free to go hand-held wherever and whenever you want.

MORE ABOUT THAT SHOT-LIST

Remember that shot-list in the chapter on "Directing"? When choosing shots, don't think of pans, zooms and booms. Think of your story first. When deciding how to shoot a scene, ask yourself, "What is the purpose of the scene?" Once you are able to define that purpose clearly, then making a shot list is nothing but a bunch of fun.

Remember, the shots are not for the sake of the shots. The shots are for the sake of the story. If your story calls for a boom shot, then let it be a boom. But don't boom just to boom. To pan just to pan is no plan. Think of the needs of your story first, and your honest shots will follow!

Now go get that camcorder and practice!

Notes:

Lighting

In order to a get a picture onto video tape, we must have light.

When making movies, we're either making light, or controlling light.

When it comes to making light outside, God has already taken care of that. It's called the sun. Rises every morning. Sets every afternoon. But if the sunlight is causing unwanted shadows on the face of the actor, we control that light—using aluminum foil, white poster paper or your favorite old white bedsheet.

CONTROLLING LIGHT OUTSIDE

The easiest way to control sunlight is to let nature do it for us, through cloud cover. Hollywood calls thick cloud cover "God's silk." Cloud cover diffuses the sunlight. If God's silk is not working, though, Hollywood builds overhead frames that hold a large piece of silk or a large mesh net. These silks or nets soften and diffuse the sunlight.

In our program, we don't have large overhead silks, so we'll use other ways to diffuse harsh sunlight. As mentioned, the best way is to shoot on a cloudy day. One word of warning about clouds, though: If you're shooting on a day when the clouds cover, then break up, you may run into trouble matching shots in editing. Let's say that you shoot your master shot when the clouds are overhead. The light is soft on your actors. When you shoot your close-ups, though, the sun breaks through the clouds, creating bright light and shadows on the actors.

When you get to the editing room, you cut from your master shot to your close-up, but the light in the close-up does not match the light in the master shot.

One way to solve the problem is to hold a large white sheet over the actors when you shoot the close-ups. The white sheet could act like an overhead silk and soften the sunlight, allowing the master and close-ups to match.

Have you ever seen those black nets gardeners use to create shade over light-sensitive plants? They're called "shade-cloth." Shade-cloth hoisted over your actors can diffuse harsh sunlight.

If neither the white sheet nor the shade-cloth works, go ahead and shoot your close-ups. You will notice a difference in lighting as you cut from the master to the close-ups, but it doesn't matter in this program. We want you to be aware of the concept of matching light, from shot to shot. But if you can't do it, keep shooting. Experiencing the problem will teach you the lesson. Some lessons in movie making are hard to envision until they are encountered.

Another way to diffuse harsh sunlight is to shoot in the shade. Could you rewrite your scene to take place under shade trees?

CONTROLLING LIGHT WITH REFLECTORS

If a large white sheet and shade-cloth diffuse sunlight, other tools can reflect, or bounce, sunlight.

Let's say your character is standing in a field. The sun offers a nice key light on one side of the actor's face. But, the other side of the actor's face is in shadows. In this case, you need a fill light, just as the name indicates, to "fill" the shadows. You can get that fill light by bouncing (or reflecting) light from the sun.

The best homemade material for reflecting sunlight is aluminum foil. Stretch the foil across a piece of cardboard, as large or small as you need. Use the dull side of the aluminum foil to create soft bounced light. Use the more reflective side of the aluminum foil for a brighter fill. White poster paper can also bounce light.

Let's imagine a situation where the actor's eyes are set in shadows. The aluminum foil reflector can fill those shadows. Here's how it works:

When you're ready for the shot, have a member of the crew stand out of frame with the aluminum foil reflector. Hold the reflector at an angle that captures the sunlight while bouncing it back into the actor's face. If the light is too harsh, have the crew member back away until the light is right. Light reflected into the eyes of the actor may cause the actor to squint. Move the reflector around in an effort to fill the shadows without making the actor squint.

LIGHTING INTERIORS

Lighting inside is the same concept as lighting outside. Outside, our key light (the main source of light) is the sun. Inside, we make our key light, using electricity. Then, we make another light to fill the shadows created by the key light. Where do we begin?

We begin with the script and the actors. Watch the actors rehearse the scene with the director. The director decides upon the camera position for the first shot. Once we know the camera position—and where the actors will sit, stand and move in the scene, we're ready to light.

The first thing we do is put up a key light, the main source of light in the scene. One promise of this training program is to teach you to make a movie, using equipment you already own. You already own reading lamps, floodlights, etc. These lights can help you achieve dramatic lighting. The "scoop" light that comes with a "scissors" clamp attached works well. Every household has one or two in the basement or garage. If not, you can get them at your local hardware store for a few dollars. They hold different size flood-lamps and can clamp to things like a door, an overhead beam, a stepladder or to a 2x4 board your crew might rig as a "light stand." Be aware that when you buy flood lamps, they come in "flood," "spot," and "narrow spot." You might need a "flood" for your fill light, a "spot" for your key light and a "narrow spot" for your rim light. Experiment to see which lamp gives you the lighting pattern that you need.

LIGHTING THE INTERIOR SCENE

When you light a scene, think in terms of building light, like building blocks, adding one light at a time.

THE KEY LIGHT

Stand back and look at the set. Decide where you want the key, or main source of light, to be in the shot. The key light will be the brightest point in the shot. The audience's eye will be drawn to the brightest point. That may be one fac-tor that helps you decide where you want your key light to be. (Don't set the key light right beside, or right behind the camera. It makes the lighting look harsh, like the evening news. Set the key light off at an angle, to one side of the camera, or the other.)

Once the key light is set, turn it on. Observe the effect the key light has on the set and the actors. If it's creating harsh shadows, raise it up. Raising the key light should throw those shadows onto the floor.

Once the key light is raised, it should be high and pointed down on the actors at about 45 degrees. If you can't get that, though, put the key light wherever it gives you the result that you want. If it's too bright on the actors, back it off. If it's not bright enough, move it closer.

Notice the light on the actors' faces. Notice that the key light has created shadows on the other side of their faces. It's time to fill those shadows with light.

THE FILL LIGHT

You started with the key light. Now it's time to build, adding another light—the fill light.

If the key light is to the right of the camcorder, set the fill light to the left of the camcorder. The purpose of the fill light is to fill the shadows created by the key light. Turn the light on, point it at the actors and move it around. Moving the light around helps locate a place where the light fills the shadows. When you find that spot, clamp the light in that position.

The fill light should not be as bright as the key light. If the fill light's job is to fill shadows, you don't want an intense fill light creating unwanted shadows of its own. If the fill light is too bright, back it away. Or, you can bounce the fill light. Bounced light makes a nice soft fill light that works great on actors.

To bounce light, spring clamp a piece of white poster paper to a chair, a ladder, or anything that will hold it in place. Spring clamps from your local hardware store are the same clamps they use in Hollywood. Position the white poster paper near the spot you want to fill. Blast your light into the white poster paper. The light bounces off the poster paper and softly fills the shadows on the actors' faces. (A piece of foam core, from your local art supply store, works well to bounce light. It costs more than poster paper, but it's rigid, so it stands up by itself.) Move the white poster paper around until the shadows created by the key light are filled.

By now, you have a key light and a fill light. Next, let's set a rim light.

THE RIM LIGHT

The rim light comes in behind the actor, striking the actor on the "rim" of the shoulders. It's sometimes called a "kick" light—because it "kicks" the actor in the back of the head. The rim light outlines the shoulders and helps separate the actor from the background. It is not necessary that you use this light at your level of training, but you should be aware of what the rim light does. When you watch Hollywood movies, observe the shoulders of the actor to see if you can see the rim light working.

THE BACKGROUND LIGHT

The last "basic" light we'll talk about is the background light. Turn on the key light, the fill light, and the rim light, then simply look at the background. Does it need light? If so, how much? Where, on the set, could you hide a light that would throw light on the background without creating unwanted shadows? Once you find that spot, set the light. If it's too bright, back it off. If you can't move it, try diffusing the light with silk or wire mesh screen over the front of the light.

CONTROLLING LIGHT INSIDE

Inside, we make light. We also control light. If one of your lights is too bright, "punch" it through an old piece of silk, old hosiery, or through a piece of tracing paper purchased from your local art supply store. Tracing paper is excellent material for softening light, but be careful not to let the lighting instrument touch paper or fabric. It could start a fire. Remember that shade-cloth we used outside to diffuse light? Cut off a piece, staple it to a frame, and "punch" the light through the net. (Any time you use cloth as diffusion, build some kind of frame to hold the cloth.)

Wire mesh can be gaffer-taped over a scoop light to diffuse harsh light. In Hollywood they call wire mesh in front of a light a "scrim." Scrims cost money. In our program, wire mesh over a light can be a piece of your Uncle Fred's old window screen—and it's free. The wire mesh kitchen utensil used to keep grease from popping from a frying pan can diffuse light. (In fact, in case you wondered, that's what the girl is holding on the cover of the book.) Another way to control light inside, as has been discussed, is to bounce the light, using white poster paper or foam core.

There is a fixture that goes on the front of a light in Hollywood called the "barn door." They're called "barn doors" because they, literally, look like doors on either side of the lighting instrument. Barn doors are used to block light off an area in the shot where it is not wanted. Your version of a barn door can be a piece of cardboard, spray painted black. Have a crew member hold the cardboard wherever it is needed in front of the light, to "barn door" the light off whatever you don't want the light to be on.

Another tool that is valuable during the production phase of movie making is gaffer's tape. It is a wide, cloth-backed tape that looks like duct tape, but it's not duct tape. Everything in the production phase of movie making is temporary. We tape aluminum foil to lights, etc. After production, we un-tape. Duct tape tends to gum up with heat and not come off easily. The best tape to use during production is gaffer's tape. Gaffer's tape is sold in professional supply stores. If there's not one in your area, we'll offer a supply house for that sort of equipment on our website at www.makeamovie.net.

WHEN ACTORS MOVE

It's one thing to light a group of actors who are sitting still. When actors move, though, lighting gets more complicated. The common sense way to think of it is that when an actor moves out of one light, he must move into another light. Watch where the actors move during rehearsal and set lights for where they move. Don't worry about key, fill and rim. Just put up a light where the actor moves. If it's too bright, either back it away, bounce the light or punch it through some kind of diffusion.

THE CHINESE LANTERN

The Chinese lantern is a terrific way to light moving actors. You'll need a light socket on the end of a long electrical cord. Get a dowel pin, or a wooden mop handle—any kind of pole as long as it does not conduct electricity. Dangle the light socket from the end of the pole, the length you need, then tape the electrical cord to the end of the pole. Tape the electrical cord all the way down the pole, so the cord will not get in the way. At this point, you have a light socket dangling from the end of a long pole. Add the size bulb you think you need for your scene, then enclose the bulb with a white Chinese lantern, which you can purchase from your local import store. Using the Chinese lantern, you have instant light—and instant diffusion.

When you're ready to shoot, have a crew member hold the lantern out toward the actors (out of frame, of course). When the actors move, the lantern can move along with them, bathing them in soft light. Be sure to follow manufacturer's instructions when using the Chinese lantern.

MIXING SUNLIGHT AND ELECTRIC LIGHT

Let's flash back to the lesson on color temperature. Sunlight offers a blue cast to a photograph. Tungsten light offers an orange tint. The professional would say you're not supposed to mix sunlight and tungsten light. We're going to anyway.

Let's say you have a scene that takes place at a kitchen table. There is a window next to the table that provides a perfect key light for the scene. The key light, in this example, is the sun. Let's say that to "fill" the shadows on the actor's face, you use a scoop light with a tungsten bulb. Your key light is sunlight. Your fill light is tungsten. In this situation, you have mixed the "blue" of sunlight with the "orange" of tungsten. The professional would not do this. It might cause an orange tint to the actor's skin tone—or an overall blue tint to the picture, depending upon if you set your camcorder for tungsten or sunlight.

Even though the professional would not mix sunlight and tungsten light, we will. Our goal is to light our scene as best we can and make a movie. Whatever methods allow us to reach that goal, as long as they are safe, are fine. We make movies with the equipment we have. Set your camcorder for the dominant light in the scene (in the example above, it would be sunlight), white balance your camera and tell your story.

SAFETY

The most important thing about lighting is safety. Lighting requires electricity, and electricity can be dangerous. A responsible adult should always be present when working with electricity. This training program is not designed to teach the rules of safety, regarding electricity. Before working with electricity, seek guidance and safety instruction from a licensed electrician.

PUT LIGHTS WHERE YOU WANT LIGHT

When I started learning about lighting for movies, it was all very confusing. People would talk about the percentage of light that "had" to come from the key light—and the percentage of light that "had" to come from the fill light. That's all a lot of baloney. I want to save you the pain of that confusion. The best advice I ever had on lighting was to decide how you want the scene to look, then start building lights in an effort to achieve that look.

We've talked about how to build the lights, beginning with the key light, then the fill light, the rim light then the background light. This is basic lighting, but it is not a formula. You should not think you have to go by a formula. Part of being a student is exploration. Imagine how you want the light to look in your scene, then try to create that light. Start with your key light. Every situation has a main source of light. Once you have established that main source of light, start adding lights, exploring, discovering how to create the look that you want.

YOUR LIGHTS ARE SET

Once the lights are set, call the actors back onto the set. Watch them through the camera as they step through the scene. If you need to adjust a light, do it now.

Look through the camera. Do you see light stands or cables in the shot? If so, "dress" them out of the way.

Once the lights are as good as they're going to get (for this movie anyway), take a deep breath, smile and tell the director you're ready. When the director says, "Roll camera," turn on the camera. You're making movies.

Notes:

Sound

When you see a good movie, you don't notice the sound. Good sound does not call attention to itself. As movie makers, we want to move an audience through an emotional experience. Good sound should blend into, and become part of, that experience.

Dialogue is only one type of sound that makes up the experience of what you hear at the movies. Other kinds of sound are:

1) Sound effects. Edited into the movie during post production.

2) Voice-over narration. If your story requires a narrator, to tell parts of the story, that voice-over (V.O.) is recorded later, not on-camera during production. Voice-over is added to the sound track in post production.

3) Foley. A Hollywood term, probably named for the pioneer who started it. Foley refers to sound effects created in post production especially for the movie by a foley artist. (We'll talk more about foley later in the chapter on editing.)

4) Music is another part of the motion picture sound track. When your movie is edited, watch it with no music. Then add the music and watch it again. Music can be magic. It can help bring a movie to life.

5) Dialogue (location sound recording): Most of this chapter will concentrate on learning how to record good dialogue, on location. We'll call our crew member who records location sound the "Sound Person."

RECORDING DIALOGUE ON LOCATION

Recording location sound for a movie is simple. It's the problems that make it challenging. In this chapter we're going to talk about how to record location sound and how to deal with some of the problems that accompany location sound.

THE TWO MOST IMPORTANT RULES FOR RECORDING SOUND ARE:

1) Proper microphone selection.

2) Proper microphone placement.

There's no need for a full lesson on how sound is created and why we hear. But, in order to better understand microphone selection and placement, let's review the basics.

Imagine that a plate falls onto the floor. Sound waves are created when the plate strikes the floor and, like waves on a pond, they ripple out in all directions. Those sound waves travel to an ear, which, working together with the brain, translates the sound waves into an impulse that a human, or some other living creature, can hear.

The microphone is a mechanical ear, capable of picking up sound waves and translating them into an electrical impulse that can be recorded onto magnetic or digital tape.

There are three types of microphones, each capable of recording sound in different directions, called "pickup patterns." When you choose a microphone, you are choosing a pickup pattern. That's why microphone choice is important.

If you want to record traffic noise, you might choose a microphone that picks up sound in all directions. On the other hand, if you want to record an actor speaking, and not record the extraneous sound around the actor, you would choose a microphone with a narrow pattern that would pick up in the direction of the actor, but not in other directions.

There are three basic pickup patterns. The type of microphone is named after its pickup pattern.

The omni-directional microphone. "Omni" means "all." The name "omni" indicates that the pickup pattern of the omni microphone is all directions, to the front, sides and below the microphone.

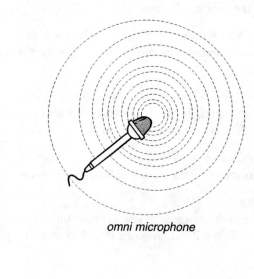

omni microphone

The shotgun (directional) microphone. This pattern reaches out, picking up sound in the direction it is pointed.

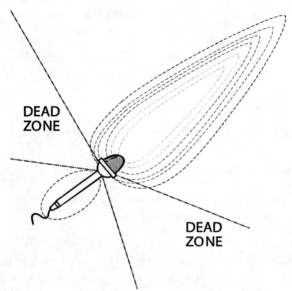

The cardioid mike. "Cardioid" means heart. The name indicates that this microphone has a pickup pattern shaped like a heart.

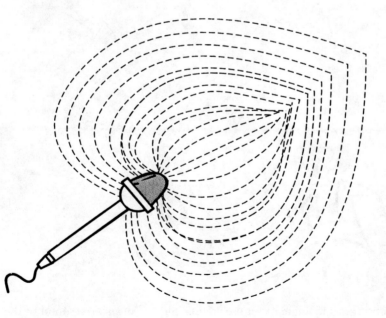

Sound people in Hollywood consider the cardioid their best all-around choice. It does not pick up sound in all directions like the omni. And its pickup pattern is not so critical that it has to be pointed directly at the actor at all times. There's room for error.

The cardioid also has a reputation for recording good voice tones. If you're only able to get one microphone, get a hand-held cardioid mike. There is also a cardioid lavaliere, the clip-on microphone you see in television news interviews.

In recording sound, you will choose, depending upon the pickup pattern you need, an omni, shotgun (directional) or cardioid microphone. Or, you may choose a lavaliere microphone, with a cardioid or omni pickup pattern.

MICROPHONE PLACEMENT

The closer you position the microphone to the source of the sound, the better the sound.

But it has to be the right microphone.

Think of the microphone as having an attached "pickup pattern." The goal is to get that pickup pattern as close to the source of the sound as possible.

If you can't get close to the actor, you may need a shotgun microphone. The shotgun's pickup pattern will reach out and capture the actor's voice without also picking up a lot of extraneous sound. If you use an omni microphone, you will pick up the actor's voice and every other sound around and behind the microphone, too.

This brings us to "signal-to-noise" ratio. "Signal" means the sound of the actor's voice. "Noise" means the extraneous background noise. If you hold a microphone two feet in front of an actor and record that actor's voice, you will record a strong "signal." If you listen carefully to that recording, you should not hear much background sound, or "noise." That means you have a good "signal-to-noise" ratio. (Good voice, "signal," low background sound, "noise.")

If you move that same microphone back twenty feet and record the same actor delivering the same lines at the same level, you will notice a higher level of background noise. This would be a bad signal-to-noise ratio.

We want a good signal-to-noise ratio. To get that. . .

1) We choose the microphone with the pickup pattern that best meets our needs under the given circumstances.

2) We place that microphone as close to the actor's voice as possible while making sure that the camera does not see the microphone, not even a shadow of the microphone.

Hiding the microphone is part of the fun of movie making. You'll hide microphones in plants, under tables, and behind lamps. You'll decide to direct a scene in a creative way, just to get the actor to talk in a certain direction—because that's the only place you could hide the microphone.

When shooting a scene with George Burns, the Hollywood sound person couldn't find anywhere to hide the microphone. He ended up hiding a small microphone in George Burns' cigar. Hiding the microphone is part of the creative challenge of getting good location sound.

THE BOOM POLE

This training program is about using equipment you already own, or can borrow. A boom pole is nothing more than a way to get the microphone out to the actor, for optimum microphone placement. A professional boom is made of light-weight material because the "boom operator" has to hold it over his head all day. For our purposes, though, any kind of pole that gets our microphone into position will be fine, a cane pole used for fishing, or a long broom handle. The only requirement is that it get the microphone into position, hold it steady, and allow the boom operator to adjust the mike toward each actor as they deliver their lines.

Any of these microphones can be purchased from your local electronics store, or your school may already have one. If so, make sure the jack is the right size to plug into your camcorder. If it's not, an adapter may work.

The microphone should be attached to the boom pole in a secure manner (not dangling by a microphone cable) so when the boom is adjusted, the microphone will adjust with it, in the direction the boom operator is pointing the microphone.

The boom operator should be aware that if he bumps the boom pole, that "bump" could pick up on the microphone. To avoid this problem, place a piece of foam between the pole and the microphone, then tape the microphone securely to the pole. The foam will act as a shock mount for the microphone.

THE SOUND RECORDER

Working with film, Hollywood records sound directly to a tape recorder, which runs in perfect sync with the motion picture film camera. In video, sound is recorded directly to the same videotape that also records picture.

Check the manual that came with your camcorder to learn how to record sound on your particular camera. There may be a control on the side of your camcorder that will allow you to adjust your record level. In most camcorders, though, the record level is monitored automatically.

Monitoring the record level manually is called "riding sound." "Riding sound" means adjusting the record level up or down as needed. If the sound person knows, for example, that, at a certain point in the scene the actor will shout, he can anticipate when that will be and adjust the record level down just as the actor is about to shout—so the "shout" will not cause the sound to distort. If you can "ride" the sound level manually, do so. If not, your sound levels will be monitored automatically.

LET'S RECORD LOCATION SOUND

The camera is loaded. We have our script. The actors are prepared. We're ready to record location sound. The first thing we do is look at the needs of the scene.

On the set, the director rehearses the actors. During the rehearsal, the sound person should observe where the actors sit, stand, move—and in which direction they speak when delivering lines. Once the sound person knows this information (and where the camera will be placed), she is ready to choose which microphone she will use and where that microphone will be placed. Only by knowing what the camera will "see" in the scene, can the sound person choose the proper microphone placement. Remember, the camera should not see the microphone, or even a shadow of the microphone.

When the actor speaks, the voice waves move out from the face and instantly spread upward and downward. Because of the direction voice waves leave the face, optimum microphone placement is two to three feet in front of the actor and slightly above or slightly below the actors' face.

If the actor is walking and you're picking up footsteps, mike the actor from below to avoid those loud footsteps.

Watch the rehearsal and ask yourself, how can I get a pickup pattern close to the actor's voice waves without the camera seeing the microphone, or a microphone shadow?

This is where the fun starts.

Let's say you have a master shot with two people seated at a dining room table. It's a wide shot, leaving a lot of space between the top of the actor's head and the top of the frame. You have your cardioid microphone attached to the end of your cane pole, but, in order to get it close enough to the actors, the camera will see the microphone.

So, where do you put the microphone?

You could choose another microphone. What about a lavaliere? You could clip the lavaliere inside the shirt of actor A and run the cable under the table, back to the camera. That would be fine if actor A is the only actor speaking. But what if both of the actors speak? The lavaliere might be good for actor A, but not good for actor B, who is seated across the table.

Let's go back to the cardioid microphone already attached to your cane pole. You can't get that mike close enough from the top. Can you get it close enough from the bottom? Nope. The actors are seated at the table, and the table will block the sound from reaching the microphone.

What are we going to do? How about this: We could ask the Art Department to put a flower arrangement on the table. The sound person could get down behind the table, hold the microphone behind the flowers and turn the microphone toward each actor as the actor delivers his or her lines. If that won't work, because we'll see the sound person in the background, we could plant the cardioid microphone right behind the flower arrangement. The heart-shaped pickup pattern of the cardioid microphone may reach out enough on both sides to pick up a good voice signal from both actors.

Place the microphone. Have the actors speak their lines at the same level they plan to deliver them during the scene. Listen through the head phones that plug right into your camcorder. Is the quality of the sound you are hearing good enough? Are you hearing the voices without a lot of background noise? If so, go with it. You have solved the problem because of your knowledge of pickup patterns.

You're not hiding a microphone. You're hiding a pickup pattern.

What else do we have in our bag of tricks?

How about a microphone with a different pickup pattern, like the shotgun mike? The pickup pattern on the shotgun can reach out to the actors. We could fix the shotgun mike to the boom and hold it further back, out of frame, and still get a good signal-to-noise ratio. Because of the narrow pickup pattern, the shotgun microphone must be aimed directly at the actor who is speaking.

We don't hide a microphone, we hide a microphone pattern.

MICROPHONE SELECTION IS A COMPROMISE

For every plus in microphone choice, there's a minus. While the far-reaching pickup pattern of the shotgun helps us solve our problem, it can present us with another problem. Because the pickup pattern is narrow, it must be aimed fairly accurately at the actor who is speaking. Let's say, for example, that the actor suddenly stands while delivering his line. The sound person would have to anticipate this sudden move and adjust the microphone, or the actor would be "off-mike" when he speaks. This is something to be aware of when using a shotgun mike. One of the jobs of a good boom operator is to anticipate the actor's moves and adjust the microphone accordingly.

The shotgun microphone does a great job of picking up sound in a specific direction. That's the good news. The bad news is that it picks up everything in that direction. Let's say you're recording an actor outside using the shotgun mike. You're getting his voice fine, but—in the distance, behind the actor, you're also picking up traffic noise.

When recording location sound, you need to consider all the circumstances, then make the best choice you can regarding microphone selection and microphone placement.

SOUND PERSPECTIVE

We want to place the microphone as close to the source of sound as possible, but not if it doesn't sound right for the given circumstances. Let's say you have a situation where two people are in a wide shot across a large, empty room. You are able to hide a microphone two feet from the actor who speaks. But, would it sound right for the actor, from that far away, to be speaking with that clear a voice signal? No. The voice would sound closer than the actor delivering the lines. The sound perspective would not be realistic.

On the other hand, if you pull the microphone back, you will get a boomy, hollow sound because your microphone placement is too far away. That's not true sound perspective either. Experiment to find the sound level that your sense of truth tells you is right. As the actors rehearse their lines, move the microphone around until you find a level that sounds right for the given circumstances. Place your microphone there.

IS YOUR LOCATION "LIVE" OR "DEAD"?

In a "live" room, the sound bounces off the hard, flat surfaces, making a hollow sound. In a "dead" room, sound waves are absorbed by cushions, carpets or drapes. It usually works better to record sound in a "dead" room.

If we have a "live" room, we can make it "dead." Furniture pads are great for deadening a room, as long as they're not seen on camera. Bring in an old carpet. Close the curtains. Throw pillows around. Be creative. Use your own good common sense to create a room that will absorb sound waves, rather than bounce sound waves.

WIND NOISE

If wind blows into the microphone, it makes a roaring noise. One of the methods used to control wind noise is foam rubber around the microphone. Don't use a thick foam that might block the sound waves from reaching the microphone. Use something porous, so the sound waves can get through. How about stuffing a boot sock with cotton, then covering the microphone with the stuffed sock? If you don't want to make one, you can buy a "wind sock" at your local electronics store, made to fit right over your microphone.

BACKGROUND NOISE

Background noise is one of the biggest challenges in recording good location sound. Even the most experienced Hollywood professionals wrestle with background noise every day. The film studios in Hollywood have sound stages. The name comes from the fact that the stage walls are padded so the sound won't bounce. And, the walls are thick enough to block out extraneous noise from the outside world. If you're shooting on a sound stage and an airplane flies over, no problem. If a siren goes by, no problem.

When we go on location, though, there are all kinds of sound problems we have to solve. The first way to solve the problems is to avoid noisy locations. We would not want to choose a location near an airport or a highway. There would be no way to stop the noise. Don't try to make yourself believe that, since we might see the source of the noise in the background, it would seem natural in the scene. The background noise would not match in editing.

BACKGROUND NOISE AND EDITING

Let's suppose that we are shooting our master shot in the middle of an open field. Looks quiet enough. But, then, right in the middle of the scene, a plane flies over. After the "take" is complete, you decide the voices were fine—and the sound of the airplane will not be a problem.

But consider this: After shooting your master scene, you go in for close-ups. In the close-ups, you want the actors to match the dialogue from the master scene. But, now, in the close-ups, the sound of the airplane is not present. In editing, you have a master shot with the sound of the airplane in the background. When you cut to your close-ups, though, the sound of the airplane is noticeably missing. This will cause a sudden change, or drop-out, of background sound that your audience will notice.

Let's say, in a different situation, that you are shooting a scene by a stream. Your microphone choice is right for the situation and the placement of your microphone is fine, giving you a good signal-to-noise ratio. As long as the audience sees the stream, at some point, they will know what the "gurgling" sound is and they will accept it.

As far as the background sound is concerned, it's not a problem similar to the airplane—because the background sound will be consistent. When we go in for close-ups, after the master, the stream will continue to make the same consistent "gurgle." In editing, the background noise in the master shot and in the close-ups will match.

BACKGROUND NOISE: BE A CREATIVE PROBLEM SOLVER

Try to pick locations where there is no background noise, or where you can control the background noise. But, if you can't be choosy, be a creative problem solver. I was directing a film once where we were shooting in an old western town. The location provided us with a wild west jail, a turn-of-the-century barber shop and a sheriff's office. It was the perfect location except for one thing—there was a small herd of sheep nearby. All they did all day long was bleat. There was no way we could shoot a scene without the sheep making noise. We didn't have time to haul them away for the day, so we got creative.

We chopped leaves off nearby trees and piled the leaves just outside the sheep's corral. Production assistants stood by on "sheep patrol." When the actors were ready, I told "camera" and "sound" to roll. Then, right before calling "action" for the actors, I would shout, "Feed the sheep." The instant those leaves were fed to the sheep, the sheep starting munching and we able to shoot. At the end of the scene, after I called "cut," we would shout, "Stop feeding the sheep." It went on like this all day, and we got every shot we needed, right on schedule.

BACKGROUND NOISE THAT HUMANS DON'T HEAR

We hear background noise all day long. We're not always aware of these sounds, though, because our brain has a way of editing out sounds we don't need to hear. Right now, the air conditioner may be on in your house. Are you aware that you're hearing it? One of the magical things about the human brain is that it allows us to concentrate on our task at hand by blocking out a certain level of unwanted background noise.

But the microphone does not have as selective a brain as humans have. The microphone hears everything. If you shoot a scene with the air conditioner running, the microphone will pick it up and record it. If it does not hear the sound of the compressor itself, it will "hear" the sound of the air "shushing" through the vents.

As a sound person, you will be faced with a dilemma. If you shoot your master shot with the air conditioner on, you must match that background noise when you shoot your coverage. But, air conditioners turn on and off. What if it's off when you're ready for the coverage?

If you use a location that has background noise, try to find a location where you can at least control the background noise. The best way to handle air conditioners is to deal with the problem before it starts by picking a location where you can control the air conditioner.

1) With the air conditioner on, prepare your scene, set the camera, hang your lights, rehearse your actors, place your microphone and set your sound levels.

2) When you are ready to shoot, turn the air conditioner off. Shoot the master.

3) When you are ready to move in for coverage, turn the air conditioner back on and re-light for the coverage.

4) When you're ready to shoot the coverage, turn the air conditioner off—and shoot.

There's a trick to hearing background noise. Plug one ear with a finger. This "short-circuits" the brain's ability to edit out background noise, allowing you to hear what the mechanical ear of the microphone will hear.

In shooting location sound, we will never be able to control all of the background noise. Even the most expensive Hollywood productions are forced to deal with chirping birds, airplanes, and noisy cars. All we can do is try to creatively solve the problem, based on our knowledge of microphone pickup patterns and microphone placement.

Let's say we're shooting a scene in a park. There is traffic noise on a nearby street. Because the actor is so far from the camera, we choose the shotgun mike to record dialogue. The shotgun mike picks up the actor's voice fine. But, the shotgun also picks up the traffic noise in the distance, behind the actor. How can we solve this problem? If we've done our homework on pickup patterns, we know that the shotgun microphone has a narrow (and long) pickup pattern to the front but no pickup pattern to the rear. If we re-stage the scene, we can aim the shotgun mike directly toward the actor, while also positioning the traffic noise to the rear of the shotgun microphone. This will give us a good voice signal from the actor and the traffic noise will be cut to a minimum. By understanding pickup patterns, we can solve recording problems.

ADR (AUTOMATIC DIALOGUE REPLACEMENT)

ADR is a Hollywood term that stands for "Automatic Dialogue Replacement." If there is dialogue that is unacceptable because of background noise, ADR can replace that unacceptable dialogue later in post-production.

The actor watches himself deliver the line on screen, complete with unacceptable background noise. With the recorder rolling, the actor delivers the line again, in sync with his lips, which he sees moving on the screen. If you find yourself in a situation where you need to replace dialogue, you can give ADR a try. We'll show you how to do it in the chapter on editing. It will be difficult to get it perfect, but it will be fun and teach a valuable lesson.

If you know you're having a problem with background noise, shoot at least some of the dialogue with the actor delivering his lines while looking away from the camera, or blocking the view of his lips with a prop, a hand or another actor. Since the audience won't see the actor's lips move, replacing the dialogue later, without having to sync the new dialogue with the lip movement, will be easier.

Here's another way to replace dialogue, using a wide angle. Let's say that your script calls for two characters to be walking along a busy street, amidst traffic noise, talking. Stage the scene in a wide shot. Put the camera in the distance and pan with the actors as they walk along the sidewalk, talking. The key is to be far enough away so that the camera cannot see the actors' lips move. Later, record the dialogue in a different location, where there is no traffic noise. Then edit the new dialogue over the characters talking. Because the actors are so far away, the audience won't notice that the lip movement and the dialogue don't match perfectly. When recording the new dialogue, remember to consider sound perspective.

Let's say that most of the dialogue can be played in the wide shot, from the distance. But, there are some lines that have to be delivered in close-up. Okay. Get creative. Look at your background. What is it? Glass store fronts? If so, could you go to a quiet street in that same town that has a glass store front? Put your actor in this quiet area and shoot her close-up against that store front.

If you can't find another location that matches, go in so close with your shot that you won't see the background. Or, shoot it with a telephoto lens, throwing the background out of focus. Either of these situations may not be perfect, but they will both keep you going. Remember, the three most important words in movie production are "com," "pro," "mise."

BUT WHAT ABOUT THAT TRAFFIC NOISE?

The scene called for two people walking along a busy street, talking. If we record their dialogue in a quiet area, then add it later in editing, that's fine. But what about the realism of the traffic noise?

No problem.

We can always add "noise" to dialogue. But we cannot take "noise" out of dialogue.

After we shoot the scene with the two actors walking along the street, record a minute of traffic noise. In the editing process, after we have the dialogue edited in, we can add the sound of the traffic. Instant realism.

EXTRAS DON'T TALK

One fun thing you may not be aware of is that all those extras you see talking in the background of a restaurant scene are not really talking. Think about it. If they were really talking, their sound would be recorded onto the actor's dialogue track. Whenever you have extras talking in the background, make sure they're moving their lips, without really talking. But, for the sake of realism, they should try to make it look like they really are talking.

During the editing process, you may want to add "walla" to the scene. After you shoot your scene, record wild sound (not sync) of your extras talking to each other, saying, "Walla, walla, walla." When this "walla track" is edited in later, at a low level, it will sound like the murmur of people talking in the background.

VOICE-OVER (V.O.) NARRATION

Voice-over is recorded in a sound booth after location shooting. To create your own sound booth, first consider the problems inherent in recording sound. One problem is a "live," or bouncy room. Another problem is noise from the outside. Another challenge is microphone placement. In order to create our own booth, then, we need to create a "dead" room, away from noise, with enough room to get a microphone placed the proper distance in front of narrator.

How about a walk-in closet? The hanging clothes absorb the sound. If there are flat, hard surfaces, you can cover them with pillows. Is this house next to a busy street? If so, you may have trouble, even though you're inside the house. An especially bad place to record is near a traffic light on a major street. Everything is quiet. Your actor is doing great, then, suddenly, the light turns green and twenty cars roar away from the light. Acting is hard. Don't make it more difficult by forcing the actor do multiple takes because of outside noise. Find a "dead" closet on a quiet street with an air conditioner you can control. Make sure the closet has plenty of headroom for the microphone. It's best to leave the actor in the booth alone. If the director and sound person are there too, there's more chance for extraneous noise. The director and sound person can work outside the closet. Run the cable under the door. Also, the actor will need a light in the "booth" to read the narration. The actor should be aware not to turn script pages while reading. The mike will pick up the sound of the page turning. Pause, then turn the page.

If you can't find a closet, a bedroom with lots of drapes and carpet should be fine.

Be creative. Use what you have.

SOUND EFFECTS

Recording sound effects can be fun and inventive. Remember the movie *Jaws*? There was that famous, eerie sound when the shark bumped his nose against the boat. The sound person who was gathering effects for *Jaws* could not find the right sound to match that action. One night he was in his claw-foot bathtub. The tub was, naturally, full of water. Sloshing around in the tub, he happened to bump his knee against the inside of the old bathtub. It made an eerie, underwater THUD. He knew that was it. That was the sound of the shark's nose bumping the boat.

You can record sound effects after the picture is edited (and you know exactly what sound effects you need), or you can record effects when you're shooting location sound. After shooting the scene, record the sound effects you want from that particular scene—like a car door slamming, or the splash of a kid jumping into the pool, etc. The good news about recording sound effects is that you don't have to worry about the camera seeing the microphone. You can get the microphone as close as you want. You can record sound effects using your camcorder, or any other device that will record sound—like a boom box.

Recording sound for movies is simple. It's the problems that arise that make it challenging. But that's part of the fun of making movies—being a creative problem-solver.

Your sound will not be perfect, but it doesn't matter. Remember, our goal in this project is not to be perfect. Our goal is to do the best that we can—and keep going.

Editing

Editing is fun. Production can be difficult. People are late. Rain falls when it shouldn't. A truck horn blares, just when your actor gets the line right. But, with editing, you're all alone with nothing to distract you. That's the good news. The bad news is, unless you're willing to re-shoot more footage, you're stuck with the footage you have. Other than that, though, editing is fun. I first knew I loved film making when I would stay up all night editing.

There is no formula to tell you how to edit. The only real rule is—tell a good story, using pictures and sound. The shots that tell your story are the shots that work. Having said that, there are editing practices that have evolved over the years. We'll talk about what they are and how you can use them to your advantage.

In the early days of motion pictures, the camera was fixed, and there was no editing. It was as if the camera was photographing a play from one position in the audience. Soon, though, silent-movie director D.W. Griffith discovered he could cut from the action in a wide shot to a continuation of that action in a close-up. Cutting to the close-up made the story more compelling. Audiences loved it. Editing changed movies forever.

As mentioned in the chapter on directing, during the days of the studio system in Hollywood, the editor worked separately from the director. The movie was shot, then sent down to the Editing Department. There was no discussion between the director and the editor. To ensure that the movie would "cut" together properly, the studio system developed a formula for "covering" the scene. The formula dictated that the director open on the master shot, go to an over-the-shoulder shot, then a medium shot, then to a close-up. With that much coverage, the studio was sure that the movie would, one way or another, cut together successfully.

Some of that old school thinking has carried over—like matching action, staying in continuity, cutting on the action and using clean entrances and exits. These time-honored rules have merit. We've already covered them in the chapters on directing and camera, but there is no way to talk about editing without bringing them up one more time.

MATCHING ACTION

If, in the master shot, the character reaches for the drink with his right hand, the character must continue to reach for the drink with his right hand in the coverage. Action must "match" from shot to shot.

SCREEN DIRECTION

If the character is facing left to right (or moving left to right) in the master, when cutting to the close-up, the character must continue to face (or move) left to right.

Screen direction for the character must remain constant from shot to shot, unless the audience sees the screen direction change. If the audience sees the screen direction change (like a car turning around), they will accept it.

HOW THE CUTAWAY SHOT CAN SAVE YOU

The editorial trick to fixing screen direction is the "cutaway" shot. Let's say you cut from a master, where the character is facing left to right, to a close-up where the character is facing right to left. This is a problem.

But, if you edit a neutral shot following the master shot—like a car approaching— then cut back to the close-up of the character facing right to left, the audience will accept this change in screen direction. Cutting to the neutral shot can cause the audience to forget the character's previous screen direction. Also, since the neutral shot comes between the master and the close-up, the change in screen direction is not so abrupt.

CONTINUITY

Think of continuity as a way to keep things on the screen "continuous." Continuity includes screen direction and matching action. Continuity also includes wardrobe, make-up and props. Let's say that, in your master shot, the actress is wearing a hat. If you cut to the close-up and the actress is not wearing the hat, that's a problem. It would be what is called a "jump" in continuity. Someone forgot to remind the actress to wear the hat during her close-up. This might be explained away by saying the character removed the hat. But that won't fly. If you cut directly from the master shot to the close-up, when did the character remove the hat?

As mentioned earlier, though, the editor is stuck with the footage the way it was shot. What's an editor to do?

The editor could try to cut to a neutral shot. The neutral shot might allow the audience to forget the character was wearing a hat in the master. If the change in continuity is not sudden, sometimes the audience will accept the change.

If you have to use the "jump" in continuity, though, use it. Making movies is a compromise. Some won't even notice the "jump."

Continuity for make-up and props follows the same logic as continuity for wardrobe. If the character's hair looks one way in the master shot, it needs to look the same way in the close-up. If a glass of milk is full in the master, it needs to be full when you cut to it in the coverage.

CUTTING ON THE ACTION

This editing technique means just what it says. When you cut from one shot to another, it's a good idea to cut on the movement, or action. If a boy reaches for a glass of milk in the master, cut to the close-up just as he reaches. If the edit is made on the action, the audience will tend not to notice the edit, providing you with that seamless flow you want your scene to have. Try it. If it makes your scene flow better, use it. If cutting on the action doesn't give you the feel that you want, then don't use it.

CLEAN ENTRANCES AND EXITS

Using the example of the boy and the glass of milk. Have the boy begin to reach for the milk in the master, then, cut to the close-up of the glass of milk. A clean entrance means the boy's hand is not in the frame when you cut to the close-up. Using a clean entrance, the boy's hand <u>enters</u> the frame. If you cut to the close-up of the milk, <u>just as the hand enters the shot</u>, it will make a smoother cut.

The same is true of a clean exit. Just when the boy's hand <u>exits</u> frame in the close-up, cut back to the master, where the action continues.

If your story-telling instincts suggest that you not use the clean entrance or exit, go with your instincts. There may be a good reason for cutting to the close-up with the boy's hand already in the frame, holding the glass of milk.

WHEN DO WE CUT TO A WIDE SHOT, A MEDIUM SHOT, OR A CLOSE-UP?

Students want to know, "When do I cut to a wide shot? When do I cut to a close-up?" There is no formula. It's story telling. Cut to the shot you need to tell your story.

To better understand the motivation for cutting from one shot to another, let's consider how we, as human beings, edit the shots we use in our everyday lives. When we go into a store, looking for, say, aluminum foil, don't we first scan the store in a wide shot, looking for the proper aisle? If we see what we think looks like aluminum foil, don't our eyes narrow to a close shot of that part of the aisle?

Let's create an imaginary situation to observe how humans see in wide shots, medium shots and close-ups.

In this situation, imagine yourself walking out of a large grocery store. You look behind you (wide panning shot). The child that was with you is no longer there. You panic as you look (medium shot) at the door of the store. Not seeing the child, you run for the store.

Inside the store (wide shot as you scan the floor, searching for the child). You run, glancing down each aisle as you go. (Dolly shot, pausing at each aisle, then continuing rapidly.) You turn the corner, frantic and see (medium shot) a child playing in the toy section. Your eyes, naturally, cut to a close-up of the child—to see if it's your child. This "close-up" reveals the face of the child.

We cut to certain shots in real life because of what we, the character, need to see in order to reach our goal within the given circumstances. Observe the shots (wide, medium, and close-up) that you use in your normal life. Note when you cut from a "wide shot" to a "close-up" and why.

There needs to be a reason to cut from one shot to another. The reason could be that the character has found his key. Cut to a close-up of the key. Or, the reason might simply be that the editor feels that it's time to cut to another shot—to pick up the pace and move things along.

In life, we cut from one shot to another for a reason. In editing we cut from one shot to another for a reason.

Warning: When making movies, you will fall in love with certain shots. Don't make the mistake of leaving a shot on the screen too long, just because you love it. The only thing your audience is interested in is the story. If your shot helps you tell your story, or if it moves the audience emotionally, stay with it. After it has served its purpose, though, move on to the next shot.

EDITING, WHERE DO WE BEGIN?

We begin where everything begins, with the script.

The editor gets the revised final draft of the script, and all the footage that has been shot, then sits down to edit the movie. The script is a guide for the editor. The editor does not have to stay, precisely, with the script. Editing is a creative process, too. The editor should ask himself, what is the purpose of the scene? If he sees a way to edit the scene that delivers the purpose of the scene in a more interesting manner than the one described in the script, then he should give it a try. The editor should keep in mind, though, that movie making is a collaborative effort. He might want to edit the "first cut" by himself, but—after that—he should be open to suggestions from the other members of the team. The "final cut" should include input from, at least, the writer and the director.

EDITING THE MOVIE

We're ready to get down to the business of actually editing a movie. This is the place where some people get nervous. I don't blame you. This technical stuff makes me nervous too. That's why I'm going to take you through the editing process one step at a time. Editing on video is not always easy, but it's simple. When you start reading through these steps, some of it may seem confusing, but it really is simple. You'll just have to patiently work through it. After a while, you'll see that it's simple. . . and fun!

Let's pretend that we shot a movie. The production phase is finished. We plan to shoot no more footage.

All our footage (ten scenes, including lots of shots in each scene) is on video tape— the kind found in any home camcorder, VHS, S-VHS, 8mm, Hi-8 or DV.

The first thing we do is plug our camcorder into our television monitor and review the footage, deciding which "takes" we like best.

Each scene on the video should be slated at the beginning of the scene, as described in the chapter on camera. The master shot should be slated, using the number of the scene. For example, the master shot of scene seven should be 7-1 on the slate. That means Scene 7, "take" 1. The coverage should be slated 7A, 7B, and so forth. 7A would be the first shot covered after the master. 7B would be the next shot covered. But this does not mean that 7A is the first shot that follows the master shot in editing. Nor does 7B necessarily follow 7A in editing. Using a letter after the number is simply a way to separate one shot from another.

THE PENCIL EDIT

After reviewing your footage, make a pencil edit. A pencil edit is a written list of the shots you want in your movie, in the order in which you want them. Go through the footage, decide which shot you want to be the first shot of your movie, then write that "scene" and "take" number at the top of your pencil edit. For example, if Scene 1, take 4 is the first shot you want in your movie, write 1-4 on your pencil edit. If your next shot is Scene 1C, take 3, write 1C-3 in the next section below on your pencil edit. At this point, you're editing the movie in your mind, imagining what these shots will look like when cut together. When you finish editing the movie in your mind, placing each shot in the order in which you want them in the pencil edit, you're ready to edit these shots together on video. (You may do your pencil edit on a legal pad, or down-load a "pencil-edit" form from the Make A Movie.Net website.)

EDITING ON VIDEO

The first two methods used to edit are Video Editing Method #1 (VEM-1), and Video Editing Method #2 (VEM-2).

Using VEM-1, you will need the same format camcorder you used to shoot your movie. You will also need one VCR with a "flying" erase head. If the VCR does not have a "flying" erase head, you will see a "glitch," or "snow," at each point where you make an edit. This is a problem we can avoid by using a VCR with a "flying" erase head.

Using VEM-1, we will record shots from the camcorder to the VCR, in the order in which we listed them in the pencil edit. We would not, of course, record the entire shot, from the slate to the end. We will, instead, review each shot, pick an in-point and out-point for each shot, then record that portion of the shot onto the VCR.

STEP BY STEP

Here's how to do it, step by simple step. If you think some of these steps are over-simplified, forgive me. I want to leave no chance for anyone to get stuck.

1) Place your camcorder onto a table next to the VCR with the "flying" erase head. Plug the camcorder into an electrical outlet. Plug the VCR into an outlet. Put a new VHS tape into the VCR. Run it forward a few seconds to make sure you're not right at the beginning of the tape.

2) Run a patch cable out of the audio and video output on the camcorder and into the audio and video input on the VCR. Audio and video are often color-coded to ensure that you patch audio to audio and video to video. If you do not have a cable, take your camcorder and VCR to your favorite electronics store. They'll help you find the right cable.

3) Run a cable out of the cable-TV plug on the back of your VCR and into the cable TV plug on your television. Plug the television into an outlet. Set the television channel on channel 3 (or whatever channel works with your VCR). Set the VCR for the channel that receives input. It will appear on the screen as AV, AUX, INPUT, or LINE 1 (Check your manual.) It's usually the channel right below Channel "2."

4) Pull up a chair, and grab your pencil edit.

5) Using the fast forward or rewind buttons on your camcorder, find the first shot listed on your pencil edit. (Do you see, now, why accurate "slates" are important during production? If you did not have good "slates," finding the shots you want, now, would be chaos.)

   Once you've found the shot, review the footage and decide where you want your "in-point" and "out-point"—the points where you want the shot to begin and end.

   Once you've made a mental note of the in-point, wind the camcorder back a few seconds, so the tape in the camcorder will be "up to speed" when it reaches the in-point.

   After you've wound back a few seconds, put the camcorder in "play," then hit "pause." The camcorder is now in "pause" mode, ready to play when the "pause" button is released.

6) Hit record on the VCR. When the VCR begins to record, hit "pause." The VCR is now in the "pause" mode, ready to record when the "pause" button is released.

7) Go back to the camcorder and release "pause." The camcorder will begin to play.

Watch your television monitor, anticipating the arrival of the in-point of the first shot. When your in-point is almost there, hit the "pause" button on your VCR. This releases the VCR to record. The VCR records, beginning with the in-point of the first shot.

Continue to monitor the shot. When you reach your out-point, hit "pause" on the camcorder. Congratulations! You just edited the first shot of your movie.

Hit "pause" on your VCR. If the shot from the camcorder recorded past your out-point, don't worry. When you cue the VCR to begin recording the next shot, you will cue the VCR at the out-point of the last shot, allowing you to record over any unwanted footage left on the end of the outgoing shot.

8) Go back to your camcorder and, following your pencil edit, find the next shot. Decide on the in-point and out-point of the next shot, rewind the camcorder a few seconds. Hit "play," then "pause."

Cue your VCR to the out-point of the preceding shot (the shot you just recorded), hit "record," then "pause."

9) Hit "pause" on your camcorder, releasing the camcorder to "play." Watch your monitor, anticipating the arrival of the in-point of this second shot. When ready, hit the pause button on the VCR. The VCR records, beginning with the in-point of the second shot.

Continue this process with every shot that follows on your pencil edit. Finally, one shot at a time, you will have edited your entire movie.

Using this method, nobody could hit each in-point and out-point perfectly. Do the best you can and be proud of yourself. You just edited your first movie.

Were you confused? If so, stand back and look at the logic of what you're doing. You're simply recording video from a camcorder to a VCR. More specifically, you are recording only the shots that you want to tell your story. It's that simple. The only hard part is the "button pushing," and you'll get used to that.

Using VEM-1, your movie will have picture and dialogue but no sound effects, music, or voice-over narration. This is fine for our training program. If you can borrow a second VCR, though, and a simple audio mixing board, you can make a movie complete with music, sound effects, foley and voice-over narration, using "Video-Method #2 (VEM-2).

VIDEO EDITING METHOD 2, VEM-2

Using VEM-2, our goal is to record from the edited VHS tape, which includes picture and dialogue only, to a second VHS tape, adding music and sound effects as we re-record.

The process is reminiscent of the old days of live television, with the crew working together to get everything right in one "pass." It may not be a perfect system, but it sure is fun—and it will allow you to make a movie that tells a story (complete with sound effects and music), using equipment you already own or can borrow.

VEM-2 requires two VCRs, an audio mixer board, and assorted cables. Check with the audio-visual department at your church or school. If they don't have an audio mixer, your electronics store will carry an inexpensive model.

Here's how VEM-2 works, step by simple step:

1) Edit your movie as described in VEM-1. You will end up with a movie (picture and dialogue only) on VHS tape.

2) Set your camcorder to the side. You are through with the camcorder for now.

3) Assemble your equipment. Two VCRs, one audio mixer board, and an assortment of cables. The cables you need will be made clear in the following steps.

4) Place the two VCRs side by side on a table. Plug them both into an electrical outlet. Label them VCR-A and VCR-B. (Using VEM #2, neither of the VCRs must have a "flying" erase head. If either has a "flying" erase head, that's fine, but it's not a requirement.)

5) Run a cable out of the video-out jack on VCR-B and into the cable TV jack on your television, or monitor. Put the channel for VCR-B on AV, AUX, or LINE 1, depending upon the instructions in the manual that came with VCR-B.

6) Our goal is to record the picture from VCR-A to VCR-B. To do that, run a cable out of the video output on VCR-A and into the video input on VCR-B.

7) Our goal is to run the dialogue from VCR-A to the audio mixer board. To do that, patch out of the audio output on VCR-A and into the audio input on the audio board. (There should be several audio input jacks on the audio mixer.)

8) Patch out of the audio board and into the audio input on VCR-B.

PREPARING MUSIC, SOUND EFFECTS AND NARRATION

Before we proceed, we need to get our music, sound effects, and voice-over narration recorded and ready for the mix. (When dialogue, music, and sound effects are mixed onto one soundtrack, it's called the mix.) Let's call the crew member in charge of this the "Mixer."

By now, the editor should have watched the movie and decided what sound effects and music will be needed.

a) The sound effects should be recorded onto a cassette tape. The sound effects should be on the cassette tape in the order in which they appear in the movie.

b) Each music selection should be recorded onto a second cassette tape. These music selections should also be in the order in which the Mixer plans to add them to the movie. (You will see, later, that the Mixer will not have time to search for the next music selection.)

c) The voice-over selections (if used) should be recorded onto a third audio cassette, in the order in which they will be added to the sound track.

d) You will need three cassette player boom-boxes, or any other piece of equipment that will play back these three separate audio cassettes. Place the boom boxes on the table next to VCR-A and VCR-B. Plug each of them into an outlet.

Patch out of the headphone jack on each of the three boom boxes and into three separate input plugs on the audio mixer. Label each of these plugs on the audio mixer as "dialogue," "sound effects," "music" or "voice-over." You should now have a set-up that looks like the diagram below:

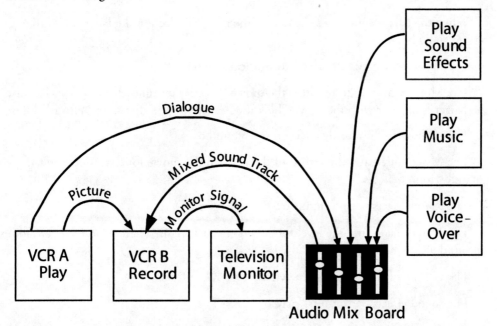

Audio Mix Board

Put one crew member on each boom box. The job of these crew members is to watch the Mixer and hit play on their respective boom box when cued by the Mixer.

The sound effects, music and voice-over cassettes should all be cued to the first "cut." Hit play for a test. Is everything plugged in and playing properly?

9) Put a blank VHS tape into VCR-B. Run it forward a few seconds to make sure it's not right at the beginning of the tape.

10) Put the edited video (completed using VEM-1) into VCR-A. Back it up a little, so the tape will be "up to speed" when the first frame of the movie begins to play.

11) Check the patch cables. If everything looks right, it's show time!

12) Hit "record" on VCR-B. When VCR-B is up to speed and recording, hit play on VCR-A. You are now recording picture from VCR-A to VCR-B. You are recording dialogue from VCR-A, through the audio mixer, to VCR-B. (Before you begin to record, make sure the dialogue level on the audio mixer is where you want it for the opening lines of dialogue.)

At this point, the Mixer should be watching the television monitor, anticipating the in-point for the first, let's say, musical selection.

When he knows the in-point is almost there, the Mixer says, "Standby for music." The crew member for music prepares. When the Mixer sees his anticipated in-point seconds away, using his own good timing, he says, "Go music." The music person hits "play" on the music boom box. The music, already cued, begins to play, recording onto VCR-B. As the music is recorded onto VCR-B, the Mixer "rides" the music level on the audio mixer board.

When the Mixer anticipates the end of the musical selection, he fades the music out on the audio board.

The music person cues up the next musical selection.

The Mixer continues to monitor the movie. Let's say a sound effect is next. Because the Mixer is familiar with the movie, he knows exactly where that sound effect belongs.

The sound effect is already cued on the boom box.

The Mixer anticipates the arrival of the place in the movie for that sound effect. "Standby sound effects."

The sound effects person stands by.

The Mixer makes sure the level for sound effects is right. There is no time for fading in sound effects.

Then, using his best timing, the Mixer says, "Go effects."

The sound effects person hits "play."

The sound effect plays, with any luck, in sync with the image on screen that, supposedly, created that sound. (After the sound effect plays, the Mixer fades "effects" to zero so the effects person can cue up the next sound effect without it being mistakenly recorded onto the video.)

The effects person cues up the next sound effect.

The Mixer watches the television monitor. What's next? Let's say it's voice-over narration.

The Mixer anticipates the point where the voice-over begins. He tells the voice-over person to stand by.

Using his own good timing, he says, "Go voice-over." The voice-over person hits "play" on the boom-box. The narration begins to play, recording onto VCR-B. The Mixer "rides" the narration level on the audio mixer board.

When it's over, the Mixer fades "narration" to zero while the crew member cues the next voice-over segment.

The "mix team" carries out this same process throughout the movie, adding sound effects, music, and voice-over where needed. Do you see how exciting this is? Do you see how important it is that everyone work together?

When it's over, fade your final music cue and cheer. You've done it. You've made a movie with dialogue, music, sound effects and, if the story calls for it, voice-over. If a few cues are "off," that's fine. Remember, our goal is not to be perfect. If you want to try it again, though, fast forward the tape in VCR-B to a fresh starting point, rewind the tape in VCR-A, and start the whole process over.

ADDING "LIVE" SOUND EFFECTS AND VOICE-OVER

There should be a place on the audio mixer board to plug in a microphone. If so, you can add the voice-over narration and sound effects "live." Kids love this because it gives them a chance to make up their own sound effects. If a bike on the screen is coming to a screeching halt, some kid will love making the sound of a screeching bike tire. Whatever creative way they want to make up sound effects is great. And they can record them right there "on the fly."

Also, it's sometimes easier for a human to match the sound effect cue more accurately using a microphone than it is to get the cue right hitting "play" on the boom-box.

AUTOMATIC DIALOGUE REPLACEMENT (ADR)

Remember, in the chapter on sound, we talked about replacing dialogue? If you shot a scene amidst loud traffic noise, for example, you might want to replace that dialogue. That can be done, using what Hollywood calls ADR, or automatic dialogue replacement. Like "live" sound effects and narration, this version of ADR is done using the microphone that plugs into the audio mixer board.

When the scene comes on-screen, the actor should be ready. As soon as the actor sees her picture begin to speak on screen, she delivers those exact same lines into the microphone, matching her voice (the dialogue) to the lip movement on screen. It's difficult, even for skilled professional actors, to match voice to lip movement on screen, so don't expect this to be perfect. But it's all part of the fun—and part of the learning experience.

FOLEY SOUND

Remember "Foley" from the chapter on sound? Foley is when a "foley artist" records sounds like feet walking and glasses "clinking" together, "on the fly," while watching the movie. Next time you watch a movie, notice the feet walking across the pavement. These "footsteps" are not recorded during production. They're created by a foley artist later in post production. The foley artist, who is often a skilled dancer, or someone with terrific rhythm and timing, watches the movie and gathers materials designed to create sound effects to match the images on screen.

The foley artist reviews the movie, making notes of the sounds she will need to create. Then, she gathers the materials needed to make those sounds. A door slamming might be a book and a board. A kid swimming might be a bucket of water to slosh her hand through. She might bring a small square of plywood to recreate the sound of footsteps on wood. Once these materials are gathered, she starts the movie, creating these sounds while, at the same time, matching them to the picture on the screen. You don't have to have a foley track, but they can be fun. You can do your own version of foley using the microphone that plugs into the audio mixer. As with ADR, it won't be easy to get the sounds to match the picture, but it sure will be fun.

TWO DRAWBACKS TO EDITING ON VIDEO

Editing on video is fine for the purposes of movie making, but there are a couple of limitations. The first is overlapping dialogue. Imagine a scene where a man is talking to a woman. The man begins to talk. Before he finishes his line, the editor cuts to a shot of the woman listening. Then, the woman begins to talk. While she's talking, the editor cuts to a shot of the man listening. This is called overlapping dialogue.

Editing on video, in the ways described, will not allow the editor to overlap dialogue. Using VEM #1, or VEM #2, we would see the man talking. When he has completed his lines, we would cut to the woman talking. When she has completed her lines, we would cut back to the man talking. Not being able to overlap dialogue is a limitation we have to accept if we're editing on video, using VEM-1 and VEM-2.

When re-recording from VCR-A to VCR-B using VEM-2, the VHS tape in VCR-B will experience a loss in picture-quality from the VHS tape in VCR-A. Simply put, whenever you copy from one videotape to another, with the exception of digital tape, you will lose some picture quality. That goes with the territory. Don't worry about it.

EDITING IN THE CAMERA

A great way to teach editing is to have your students edit a scene as they shoot the scene. This is called "editing in the camera." To do this, the student needs to storyboard each shot, either on paper or on the movie screen in his or her mind. Once the shot-list is made and each shot is planned, the shots need to be recorded in the order in which they will appear in the movie.

There will be no footage to edit out. The student will, literally, turn on the camcorder, record the first shot, from in-point to out-point, then "pause" the camcorder. The student will then reposition the camcorder and shoot the next shot, from in-point to out-point. Each shot that follows will be done in the same way. When reviewing the scene, it should look the same as if it were edited. Actually it was edited—in the camera.

Since edits are made in the camera, this requires a camcorder with a "flying" erase head, to avoid "glitches" between shots. Don't turn the camera off between shots. If you turn the camcorder off, it may cause a "glitch." That's why it's important to "pause," instead, between shots.

Editing in the camera is a great way to learn. It forces the student to plan ahead for proper screen direction, matching action, wardrobe continuity, prop continuity, clean entrances and exits and "cutting on the action."

Since all the "editing" is done in the camera, there is no need to set up editing equipment. And, if the student is prepared, it can be a quick movie to shoot, leading to immediate results which can be seen on the screen—the perfect kind of project for something like a one-hour class.

If editing on video, tape to tape, is the best you can do for now, it's perfect. If you would like to edit on computer, though, that opportunity has arrived. Editing on computer is a major breakthrough in video editing technology, allowing us to make better movies, at a lower cost, than we ever dreamed possible.

NOTES:

DIGITAL EDITING

In the earlier chapter on editing, I started by saying, "editing is fun." Let me rephrase that: Editing can be fun. When the editing process is going right, it's the same as when the writing process is going right. You're working on a scene when, suddenly, the scene speaks to you and says, "Look. Here is the real truth of me. Try it like this." And you do. And it works. Editing can be magic. Creative, sparkling magic—giving you the kind of thrill that reminds you why you wanted to make movies in the first place.

To be creative, you need to keep cooking! When you have an inspiration, you need to try it. Editing on computer gives you the power to keep cooking—to stay with that spark of inspiration and see if it works.

It's not required that you edit on computer. The promise of this book is to teach you how to make a movie, using stuff you already own. That promise is fulfilled in our belief that anyone with desire can, somehow, come up with a camcorder and a VCR. If camcorder to VCR is the only way you have to edit, then that's perfect! But if you want to explore the world of digital editing, sometimes called non-linear editing (NLE), this new technology is exciting, relatively inexpensive, and can be easy to use. Non-linear editing is another one of those technological breakthroughs that told me it was time to write this book.

Before you begin this chapter, I want you to make a promise—that you will finish this chapter. I say that because some information in the early part of this chapter can be a little intimidating, especially to a teacher new to computers. The chapter ends, though, with a simple, workable, affordable solution. My goal is to lead you through the technical forest and onto a clear, doable path. If you read this entire chapter, you'll find that path.

A simple way to describe non-linear is to make an analogy to a word processor. The word processor works with word processing software to create letters, words and paragraphs. As you know, because you've done it, those words, letters and paragraphs can be moved anywhere you want. You can cut a sentence from one paragraph and paste it into another paragraph. You can delete a word and add another word. Writing on a word processor gives you the freedom to add, delete or change words anywhere you want. A non-linear editing system (NLE) gives you the freedom to make those same kinds of changes with audio and video.

When we edit on video, tape-to-tape, we lay down one scene after another, in the order they come in the movie. This method of lining up scenes, in a linear fashion, and re-recording them, from one videotape to another, is called linear editing. Linear editing on video began because it was cheaper than editing on film, but it still has its problems.

Let's say that, using a linear editing system, we lay down a close-up of one of our characters. We look at the edit. The close-up is six seconds long. The timing seems right, so we move on. We lay down, say, twenty more shots that day—all following that six-second close-up.

The next day, we look at the scene with fresh eyes. We feel that six-second close-up is on the screen two seconds too long. We want to shave two seconds off that close-up, but — since we have been editing in a linear fashion— we can't just trim two seconds and keep going. That six-second shot is being replaced with a four-second shot. That means we'll have two seconds of empty space in our video. In order to get rid of that two seconds of empty space, we would have to go all the way back to the six-second close-up and re-record the scene (this time two seconds shorter) then re-record all of the twenty shots that followed that close-up all over again! That's a lot of work!

Instead of editing being a fun and creative process, linear editing can make it a worry. You have to worry that every shot is the right length on "the first draft"— because going back to re-edit even one shot can be time-consuming drudge work. The problem is that it's not easy to know if an edit is right that early in the process. Editing should be a creative process of discovery, like writing.

Non-linear editing gives you the freedom to discover by allowing you to start editing anywhere you want, or make changes, instantly, any place in the movie.

Not too long ago, in the film business, everything was shot on film and edited on film. Let's say you wanted a movie to end up being 48 minutes long. You might rough-cut that film to be 73 minutes. Then, the creative process would move to the next level. The rough-cut starts telling you what works and what doesn't work. You drop what doesn't work in the "first draft" and leave what does work. That's the process. That's how the movie is discovered in editing.

With film, editing was "non-linear." By that I mean that the editor could go into that six-second close-up referred to earlier, trim off the two seconds, glue the film work-print back together and keep going. Editing on film gave us the freedom to add or trim footage as needed, instantly, wherever we were in the movie.

Non-linear editing on computer gives us that same freedom. Your movie has a life of its own. It is part of your job to discover that life through the editing process. If editing were just technical, the editor could go exactly by the script, editing the scenes according to the script. But it never turns out that way. Editing is a process of discovery. Non-linear gives you the power to discover.

So how can we do non-linear editing?

Hollywood studios use expensive, computer-based non-linear editing systems. Those systems would not give you anything more, that you will really need for your projects, than you will be able to get from a much less expensive (and much easier to use) non-linear system. In fact, you can build a non-linear editing system on the computer you already have. It's not always simple, but you can do it.

TO BUILD YOUR OWN NON-LINEAR EDITING SYSTEM...

...you'll need a computer with enough RAM (random access memory) and processor speed to edit video. How much RAM will depend upon the editing software program you choose and on how large you want the picture to be on your monitor screen (1/4 screen, 1/2 screen, or full-screen.) You'll also need lots of hard drive space. How much hard drive space depends on the length of your movie (the longer the movie, the more hard drive space required); also, the higher quality picture you want, the more hard drive space will be required.

You'll also need a video digitizing board. This piece of equipment, which must be installed in your computer, turns analog video (VHS, S-VHS, Hi-8, or 8) into ones and zeroes that the computer can understand. You have to turn analog video and audio into ones and zeroes before editing on computer unless you shoot with...

THE DIGITAL CAMCORDER

Instead of creating analog picture and audio, the digital camcorder creates digital picture and audio, composed of ones and zeroes. Generally speaking, digital camcorders make better pictures and audio than analog camcorders. If you shoot all your footage in digital it's possible to get all that digital data over to your computer without a digitizing board, through a process called...

FIREWIRE

Imagine that, instead of there being pictures on that DV tape, there are a series of ones and zeroes. In order to edit those pictures, we've got to get those ones and zeroes over to your computer. One way to do that is through firewire.

Imagine that we hook a pipeline between the camcorder and the computer and we stream those ones and zeroes, like streaming water, through the pipeline, across to the computer. The pipeline, in this example, is the firewire cable. When the ones and zeroes get to your computer, the faucet that lets them into the computer is the firewire board, another piece of equipment you will have to buy if you're going to put this system together yourself.

Not all computers can handle firewire. The easiest way to find out is to ask one of the companies that sells you hardware. There are all kinds of salespeople who will tell you that it will work, but the proof is in the puddin'. Try it first. The last thing you need is a piece of equipment gathering dust in a closet.

Up to now, in order to put together your own non-linear editing system, we know you must have:

1) A computer with enough RAM and processing speed for video.

2) Lots of hard drive space. There is no way the hard drive that comes in your computer will be enough. You will have to buy extra hard drives. Plus, those hard drives must be arrayed (linked together) in such a way that they will work together, at the proper speed, to produce quality video.

3) A video digitizing board to digitize analog video.

4) If you want to stream ones and zeroes, for the highest quality video, you will need a firewire board and a computer capable of handling firewire.

While on the subject of firewire, let's make a distinction. If all the footage you ever plan to use is shot on a DV camcorder, then a firewire board will be enough. But what if, in making your movie, a student creates footage that would work well in the movie, but it was shot on S-VHS? Remember, S-VHS is analog. You will have to have a digitizing board to turn that analog into ones and zeroes. You can have a digitizing board and firewire board both in your computer. It's just going to cost you more money.

THE EDITING SOFTWARE

The hard drives, the digitizing board, the firewire board, the RAM and the speed of the computer are all hardware. The software is the brain that tells all that hardware what to do. It works the same way word processing works. Your computer does not do the word processing. Your computer works together with word processing software to make letters. Non-linear editing software works the same way.

There are several editing software packages on the market. Common sense says that if you're shopping for an editing software package, look for one that has been around for a while. Talk to other teachers who have used that exact software, on the same kind of computer that you have. Don't just talk to the media instructor at the big high school. Those teachers can be knowledgeable about editing software because they work with it almost every day, and they've learned all the tricks. It's important that you find a system that will work for you. No matter how many bells and whistles a software package claims to offer, if it's too complicated for you to use, or for your students to use, then it won't be used. If it is not used, then, needless to say, it is of no value at all.

Ask yourself what kind of editing you need to do, then shop for time-tested software that will do those things. Go to a dealer and have your own hands-on editing session, using the non-linear editing software you are considering. Take your own camcorder (and VCR) and digitize (or firewire) your own footage. Edit that footage, using every cut, fade, dissolve and titling option you will need for your movies. Once your short movie is edited, output it back to your VCR.

Was it easy? Could you do it again? How did it look? Did the quality of the audio and video meet your expectations? Will the dealer let you take the system back to your classroom, to "test drive" with your students? If so, take the dealer up on the offer. I want you to find a non-linear system that you can use, for one simple reason—I want you to use it!

"FINGER POINTING"

Finger pointing is when one company blames another for the system not working. Finger pointing is one of the dangers of putting together an NLE system yourself.

Let's say, for example, that your footage is not digitizing properly. When you get on the phone to solve the problem, the company that manufactures the digitizing board might blame the company that created the software. Then the company that created the software might blame the company that manufactured the digitizing board. Finger pointing won't solve your problem, but it will give you the sudden urge to throw the whole contraption out the window.

One way to minimize finger pointing is to make sure which products have worked well together over a period of time. Does a certain digitizing board work well with a particular software? Has a certain computer worked well with a particular brand of hard drive over a period of time?

Don't take the salesman's word for it. See it. Feel it. Touch it. Work it. Take it back to the classroom and let the students edit their own short movie. If, after a few days, you're having fun (and not pulling your hair out) you've probably got a system that will work for you.

If you want to put together your own non-linear system, with parts manufactured by different companies, you can do that. But, if you want a system where everything is put together for you, in one simple, ready-to-go box, those systems exist. One of them is called...

...THE DRACO CASABLANCA

The story goes that Eric Kloor, creator of the Casablanca, was driving down a German autobahn when one of those ideas that comes to you all of a sudden came to Eric all of a sudden. Instead of dealing with the different manufacturers that make all the different parts necessary to put together a non-linear editing system, Eric's idea was to create a non-linear editing system that comes in one simple box, with all the necessary parts and software already installed—tuned, tweaked and ready to go.

Eric came back to the U.S.A. and created the Casablanca, a complete, standalone, non-linear editing system, about the size of a VCR. The box has a digitizing board. Firewire is available. The hard drives are arrayed properly. And there are no glitches between software and hardware—because the same company created both the hardware and the software.

If something doesn't work on the Casablanca, there's only one direction to point your finger—toward Draco. To paraphrase the immortal words of Harry Truman, "The buck stops with Draco."

Before you start thinking that I own Draco, I want you to know that I don't. My goal is to get you to start movies and finish those movies. The Casablanca is the best tool I have found that gives you the power to finish your movie.

HOW I FOUND THE CASABLANCA

I knew that editing was the weak link in our movie making program, since linear editing from camcorder to VCR is so time-consuming. With that in mind, I traveled to the annual meeting of the National Association of Broadcasters (NAB) with one goal —to find a non-linear editing system that would meet the needs of our program.

1) I was looking for a system that would create high quality picture and audio.

2) I was looking for a system that was simple to use.

3) I was looking for a system that was priced so that most schools could afford it.

4) I was looking for a non-linear editing machine that was not so fragile that one impatient (or untrained) student could crash the system.

5) I was looking for a system backed by a company that would support teachers.

When I arrived on the floor of NAB, I didn't know where to begin. The convention was, literally, acres of equipment. I decided to start with a big-name company. I went to their editing section and explained what I was looking for. They ushered me over to their NLE system. It was complicated and expensive. I explained again that I was looking for something that was simple to use and affordable for most schools. The salesman listened patiently, checked from side to side as if to make sure his boss wasn't watching, then leaned forward and whispered, "Go see the Casablanca."

That's how I found Casablanca. Here's what I found:

THE CASABLANCA IS SIMPLE TO USE

"TRIM" means trim. "DELETE" means delete. "ADD" means add. There's a learning curve, but it's simple. Some functions are easier than others, but I believe most teachers and students will be able to learn the basics in a short period of time. Don't take my word for it, though. "Test drive" the Casablanca, right in your own classroom. You and your students can see for yourself.

SUPPORT

Draco has promised to offer quality support. Support can sometimes be a mirage. It's promised, but never seems to arrive. I did not want that to be the case if I recommended the Casablanca, so I spoke personally with the top management at Draco, including Eric Kloor. They assured me that every school will receive quality support, through your Casablanca dealer first, then through Draco if necessary.

PRICE

There are different models of the Casablanca and different prices. There is one priced right for you. Even if your school has no budget at all for video equipment, your movie-making program could afford to pay for the Casablanca through selling edited sports events or an edited video-yearbook. Remember, the number one requirement for movie making is desire. If your students have desire, they will find a way to pay for their NLE system.

THE CASABLANCA IS NOT FRAGILE

The afternoon class will not find that the morning class has crashed the Casablanca. You can't crash the operating system through an honest mistake.

THE SOFTWARE...

...is written specifically for the Casablanca, so there's no problem with the hardware company blaming the software company, or vice versa. The software will do every editing technique I have ever used in making movies. The software will also generate great looking titles and credits.

THE HARD DRIVES...

...are completely unique in that they pull out, like a small drawer. You can have one hard drive for the football coach and another hard drive for your movie-making program. It's a cost effective way to buy one Casablanca and have several users share the cost. By having pull-out hard drives, a school can have multiple video projects going at once, without the fear of one student deleting another student's project. Plus, pull-out hard drives guarantee you'll never run out of hard drive space—because you can always add another hard-drive.

A LITTLE ABOUT HOW THE CASABLANCA WORKS

I'm not going to write a training manual, but I would like to give you an overview of how the Casablanca works.

Plug the Casablanca into a power outlet. Plug your monitor into the back of the Casablanca. If you don't have a monitor, a television will work fine.

To describe how the Casablanca works, let's imagine a student editing a movie. Let's say she shot her movie on S-VHS. The first thing she needs to do is digitize her S-VHS footage over to the Casablanca hard drive.

To do that, she plugs her VCR into the Casablanca. It's as simple as plugging a VCR into the back of a television. She hits "PLAY" on the VCR and "RECORD" on the Casablanca. At this point, the picture and audio are being sent from the source (VCR) across to the hard drive on the Casablanca.

With the footage on the hard drive, the student is now ready to trim each shot to the length that she wants. Let's say there's a close-up of a kid looking off-screen. The editor wants to use that close-up, so she clicks on that scene in the "trim bin," the space on the monitor where the editor can see an icon of each shot that has been digitized.

She selects the close-up, then watches the shot from beginning to end. After watching the shot, she trims it to the length she wants. She doesn't have to be perfect because, using non-linear, she can easily change it later. At this point, she makes her best artistic guess as to how long she wants the shot, then she puts it into the scene.

She edits the close-up into the scene by simply clicking on the word "ADD." The editor builds her movie, one shot at a time, by trimming the shot to the length she wants, then adding it to the story board on the monitor.

Let's say that she has completed her "rough cut." She sits back and watches her movie. As she does, she notices that one of the close-ups seems, in her artistic opinion, to be a little long. No problem. This is non-linear editing. She simply stops the movie and selects that shot by clicking on it in the story board. She trims two seconds from the shot, then hits "REPLACE," and the close-up goes right back into the story board, at the new length that she wanted.

Using the Casablanca, the editor can go anywhere in the movie, trim any shot, add to any shot, delete or move any shot, from one place in the movie to another, instantly. When she has her movie like she wants it, she can hit another button and record the movie from the hard drive back out to her VCR. That's when she gets the popcorn.

The Casablanca is not the only standalone non-linear editing system, but it has the best combination of features I've found so far. It is simple to use. It is affordable to own. It is sturdy enough to stand up under lots of student use. The company that created and builds the Casablanca has an excellent reputation and provides first-rate support. All this makes me confident in suggesting that you at least "test drive" the Casablanca. It won't cost you a nickel, and it may save you lots of money (and hair) in the long run.

For more information about the Draco Casablanca, visit their website at www.draco.com or call 303-440-5311.

NOTES:

Quik Flicks

or

How to Make a Movie Fast

Teachers have time limits. You may have to get a project done in one hour. You may have a four-hour activity period available to make a movie, or you may have a day. That's not enough time to write, produce and edit most movies, but it is enough time for a Quik Flick.

A Quik Flick is a movie that tells a story. The scenes are shot in the order that they come in the movie, and all of the scenes are shot as "masters"—so there's no need for editing.

THE EXACT EQUIPMENT YOU'LL NEED

1) A camcorder, with one video cassette, charged batteries and a battery recharging unit.

2) One or two inexpensive shop lights, with small floodlight bulbs, and a few extension cords. Make sure the extension cords are large enough to carry the wattage of the bulb you're using. (If your entire story takes place outside, though, forget the lights.)

3) A microphone that plugs into your camcorder. You won't be happy with the microphone that comes connected to your camcorder.

4) Popcorn. Since we finish a Quik Flick the same day we start it, it's necessary to have popcorn standing by.

That's the equipment. You may need more in the way of costumes, props and make-up, but that all depends on the story created by your ingenious students.

CREATING THE QUIK FLICKS STORY

By now, you should have at least read the Introduction and the chapter on Story and Screenplay. A Quik Flicks story is no different from any other story. It's built by mixing the story elements of character, problem, decision and goal.

Look around you. What do you have? Where are you shooting your movie? We're going to produce this story right now, so the story has to work for the location we have. Who do we have to act? The members of your class? Great! Then we need to create a story that works for the actors and location we have available to us right now.

The basis for a story is a problem, so let's come up with a problem. Don't worry about coming up with the perfect problem. "Perfect" is the killer of creativity. Let's give ourselves permission to come up with a silly, possibly-even-bad story idea in a short period of time. If you have to make a movie in an hour, give yourself, say, ten minutes to come up with a story. If you have more time available, give yourself more time for story. Always set time limits for each stage of production. That's part of the fun of Quik Flicks. For the purposes of our example, we're going to say we have four hours for our entire production. We'll set creative time limits to meet our goal of finishing the Quik Flick within that four hours.

Ready to begin? Don't start your story conference just yet. First, send out your "story scouts."

TEN MINUTES FOR STORY SCOUTS

Get everybody ready. Set the clock. Go! For ten minutes, or whatever time limit you can afford, your students will scout the facility to see what's there. Equipment and props, like sports equipment in the gymnasium, or test tubes in the science lab can help "spark" ideas. A writer's best friend is problems. How could any of these props, locations or equipment help us get a character into trouble? At the end of the ten-minute period, the story scouts return with a list of the things they've found.

TWENTY MINUTES TO FIND THE STORY ELEMENTS

Start the clock. You have twenty minutes to come up with a main character, a problem, a goal and obstacles. What did the story scouts find? How could any combination of those props or locations help us get a character into trouble? You don't have to stick with the things the scouts found. They're only there to prime your story-idea pump. Come up with any problem that could be the basis for a story that you could shoot at this location. When the twenty-minute bell rings, you will have a main character, a problem, a decision to overcome that problem, a goal and obstacles.

THIRTY MINUTES TO MAKE A STORY

At this point, we have thirty minutes to spitball these elements into a story. The chapter "Story and Screenplay" tells you how to take these elements and turn them into a story. The thing you need to keep in mind about Quik Flicks, though, is that you must end up with a story that you will be able to produce in the time that you have.

When your story development time is up, you won't have a script. You will have a step outline, with each scene in the order in which it comes in the story—and with the purpose of each scene clearly defined.

GO TO THE LOCATION AND IMPROVISE

When you created the story, you probably came up with ideas about where you planned to shoot each scene. Also, you probably cast the movie while creating the story. So now, let's get story, cast and crew and visit each location.

Let's start with the first location. What is the purpose of the scene? The basis of every story is a problem. Likewise, the basis of every scene is a problem. What problem is at the heart of this scene? If we don't have a problem, we don't have conflict. If we don't have conflict, we don't have drama. In *Party Animal*, the problem in the first scene was that the little brother wanted to go to the party, but the big brother would not let him. What's the problem in your first scene? What does the main character want? Who or what is trying to keep the main character from getting it? Using these basics as guide posts, let the actors improvise the scene.

After the actors have had a chance to improvise, let the members of the cast and crew offer their input. We don't have time for another story conference, but we do want ideas from everyone. It's very possible that, out of this improvisation, the story will change. That happens all the time with the creative process. If you see a way to make your story better, try it. But be careful not to change the story so much that you spend all your time making changes—and you run out of time to finish your production. You want to create a story that is simple, one you are able to produce in the time that you have.

Go from location to location, in the order that they come in the outline, improvising the scenes and making notes. If a scene calls for a character to be sitting on a couch in a den at home, and you're shooting in a classroom, put chairs together and call it a couch.

When you finish improvising each scene, go back to the story table. With Quik Flicks, we don't write and memorize dialogue. Instead, write the main story points of each scene. What is the purpose of the scene? You must create the story points to fulfill that purpose. If one of the purposes of the scene is to understand that the big brother thinks the little brother will embarrass him, then you need to make sure you hit that story point in the scene.

IT'S TIME TO GET OUT THE CAMERA

Most people think that making a movie is about using a camcorder. It is, but that's the tip of the iceberg. Do you see how much time we've put into planning? I remind you of what Frank Capra said, "The key to a good production is good preproduction."

By now we've created a story and an outline. Each step of the outline represents a scene. We have improvised each scene. We understand the purpose of each scene and have agreed upon the story points that need to be made in each scene.

We have already cast the movie because we wrote the movie to fit the cast. We have already rehearsed because, during the improvisation, the actors were, at the same time, rehearsing. We're ready to shoot.

QUIK FLICKS SCENES ARE SHOT IN SEQUENCE

In almost all movies, scenes are shot out of sequence and put together in the editing room. But, with Quik Flicks, there is no editing. All of the scenes are shot in the order in which they come in the outline.

Grab the equipment. Let's go to our first location.

Once at the location, have the actors walk through the scene one more time. It's not important that they put everything into the scene emotionally. This is a chance for the director to decide where he's going to put the camera for the master shot. In the master shot, the camera will photograph the entire scene, from beginning to end.

THE ENTIRE MOVIE IS SHOT IN MASTER SCENES

When we shoot a master shot, close-ups, medium shots and cutaways, we have to be able to cut it all together in the editing room. But we don't have time for editing in Quik Flicks, so we shoot every scene in a master shot, in the order in which they come in the story.

But that does not mean that the master shots have to be boring. You can make interesting master shots! In Quik Flicks, we can't cut to a close-up in the editing room, so let's bring the close-up to us in the way that we stage the scene.

When staging your scene, put the camera in the place that gives you the best "view" of the action. When you feel it's important, dramatically, to go to a close-up, have the actress move closer to the camera. Likewise, the camera can move! You won't be able to cut to a close-up, but you can move the camera in for a close-up, or a medium shot.

Quik Flicks makes the camera a living, breathing part of the scene. The actors move. The camera moves. It's a waltz between actor and camera that tells the story of that scene.

TECHNICAL STUFF YOU NEED TO KNOW

Set your camcorder on automatic focus, automatic white balance and automatic sound monitoring. Quik Flicks are about telling a story and having fun. We'll worry about the technical details of a camcorder later.

Your goal with lighting is simply to create enough light so that the audience can see the action you want them to see. We'll worry about dramatic lighting later. Right now, just get light on the subject. If your floodlights are creating harsh shadows on the wall behind the actors, raise them higher, and those shadows will go onto the floor. Do not use electricity unless there is qualified adult supervision!

Regarding sound, get the microphone as close to the actor as possible, without letting the microphone get into the shot. It's okay if the mike gets in the shot, but do your best to keep it out. Optimum microphone placement is two feet in front of the actor and slightly above, or slightly below, the actor's face. But this is Quik Flicks. We're thinking about fun, not worrying about perfection. Position the microphone as best you can, and that will be fine. When the camera moves, the sound person can hold the boom pole for the microphone and waltz along beside the camera.

It's important to remember that, once the scene begins, you don't turn off the camera (or hit "pause") until the scene ends.

Shoot the scene from beginning to end, but you don't have to show the audience all of the action. Move around. Let the actors move in and out of the frame. Show the audience what <u>you</u> need them to see, in order to tell them <u>your</u> story.

In Quik Flicks it is a good idea to have your actors exit frame at the end of the scene. It might make cutting to your next scene work a little better. Try it and see.

MULTIPLE CAMERA TAKES

You can do multiple takes for each scene in Quik Flicks, but you'll have to rewind your videotape until you get the scene right. In other words, you shoot the first scene. If it does not go as well as you hoped, no problem! Rewind the tape and shoot the scene again, with "take" 2. When you get it like you want it, move on to the next scene. Shoot scene 2. If you need to do another "take" on scene 2, rewind the video and shoot the entire scene again. (But be careful not to rewind too much and record over the end of the previous scene.)

Shoot all the scenes in a master shot, in the order in which they come in the story. When you shoot your last master scene, hold up a card that says, "The End." Shoot five seconds of that card, then hit "stop."

You did it!

The most important thing you can do, as a movie maker, is to get into action. You just got into action—and made a movie that tells a story. Now grab the popcorn and go watch your movie.

EDITING IN THE CAMERA

There's another way to make a Quik Flick, but it requires that you write the story and plan the shots ahead of time. Once that is done, though, you can shoot a Quik Flick movie and edit it in the camera. This will allow you to cut to wide shots, medium shots and close-ups, all "edited" in the camera while you shoot.

The director designs each shot, using a storyboard. He might open on a wide shot, then cut to a close-up. Since there is no editing, he would make the movie by shooting only what he needs of the wide shot, hitting pause on the camcorder, then moving in and shooting only what he needs of the close-up. Editing in the camera requires too much planning to make up a story, plan shots and shoot the movie all in one day. That's why it's "quicker" to produce Quik Flicks in master shots that add up to tell a story.

The Hero Next Door™

*"Never doubt that a small group of thoughtful,
committed people can change the world.
Indeed it is the only thing that ever has."*

—Margaret Mead

The Hero Next Door is based on the belief that every town in the world, no matter how small, has someone who made a difference toward the quality of life in that town. *The Hero Next Door* provides an opportunity for students to discover the heroes in their own town and to make a short documentary movie about what that person did.

In the process of discovering their heroes, students will have the opportunity to learn about the history of the place they call home, while also learning that every person on earth has the opportunity to make a difference if he or she chooses to do so. It's not always easy. Sometimes it takes courage. But we all have the power to choose to do the right thing. We can't all be Abraham Lincoln or Martin Luther King, Jr., but we can all make a difference through the smallest act of courage or kindness. We may not see the results right away, but there is always a ripple effect.

Here's an example: there was a man born into slavery in Kentucky. Following the Civil War, he moved to a small town in Ohio where he farmed his own land. He worked hard, made a living and, over time, saved money. Before he died, he created a trust fund and left his life savings to that fund. The purpose of the fund was specific —

to provide money for widows to buy sugar, to bake cookies, at Christmas. For generation after generation and to this day, the trust fund has done just that. In addition to providing sugar for widows, that act of kindness has, over the years, spawned other projects in that same town—all designed to make a difference for good.

Did that man who farmed his land and started that trust fund think that what he did would be affecting lives a hundred years later? I'll bet he didn't. But it has. It affected me. His story inspired me to begin the *Hero Next Door* project. There is always a ripple effect.

Was there someone from your community who took a courageous stand during the Civil Rights movement, even though it may have been unpopular?

Was there someone from your community who knew children who couldn't read and started a literacy program?

You define "good." Whatever any person did to make life better in your community is a story that deserves to be told.

They can be stories like:

1) *The Woman Who Painted the Klan Sign Yellow.* The story of Brodie Reed, a woman who stood up to the Ku Klux Klan in a small town in Alabama.

2) *If You Can't Vote, You Can't Change.* The story of Ezra Cunningham, the first person to register African Americans to vote back in the 1950s, in the rural Alabama county where Harper Lee wrote *To Kill a Mockingbird*.

3) *Jack Smith, The Hero.* The story of an anonymous hero who started "The Friendly Supper Club" in Montgomery, Alabama, an organization designed to heal racial tensions between blacks and whites.

4) *The Job Mom.* The story of Earnestine Young, a woman who lost her leg in an automobile accident, then lost her job. Sitting at home all day, in a crime-ridden neighborhood, things seemed hopeless. At her low of lows, out of frustration, she told the teenage drug dealers on her corner that she would find them real jobs. She expected them to walk away, but—much to her surprise—they took her up on the offer. Miraculously, she found them all jobs. Word spread. In one year, the Job Mom has found jobs for 185 at-risk kids. It doesn't bring her money, but it brings her joy. And you can see it on her face in this *Hero Next Door* documentary produced by students.

The Hero Next Door is based on the belief that there are stories like Ezra Cunningham, Brodie Reed and The Job Mom in every town in the world. It is the vision of *The Hero Next Door* to find those stories and tell them to the world through short, student-produced documentaries.

Hero Next Door documentaries are simple to produce. All you need is a camcorder, a couple of lights and desire. The most important thing, as always, is desire. If you're ready, pick up your desire and let's get started.

THE FIRST THING WE NEED IS A STORY

To find a story, you need to find a "hero next door."

Sometimes students immediately jump to a person in the community who is already thought of as a "hero"—like a sports hero, or a war hero. Those stories deserve to be told, and you can tell them if you want to. But they're not exactly *Hero Next Door* stories. The *Hero Next Door* is a person who some in the community might not even think of as a hero—the little guy who stuck his neck out and made a difference. Also, *Hero Next Door* stories work best if they can be told around a specific event. If a person served the community for thirty years, don't try to make a documentary about that person's entire life. Instead, look for a specific event where he or she did something that turned out to make a difference to the quality of life in the community. The struggle around that event is your story.

INVOLVE THE COMMUNITY IN YOUR HERO SEARCH

Finding the subject for your *Hero Next Door* documentary is a great way for the school to work with the community. It's also a great way for students to learn the history that is already right under their noses. Here's one approach:

Explain the project to your students. Have them talk with their parents, grandparents, aunts and uncles. Parents and grandparents probably know a lot about the history of the community, but there may never have been a reason to talk about it. They have a reason now. And remember, the "hero" does not have to be alive today. The subject of the documentary can be from the past or the present. Who do the students' grandparents remember their parents talking about?

When students return with ideas from their families, have a story session just with the students. Invite your local newspaper to cover the story session. One purpose of the article is to include the community in the hero search. The article should ask citizens to think about someone who made a difference and should further provide a date and time for a "community story session," when those who would like to participate can come to the school with their ideas.

After the student story conference, send letters to specific people in your community. There is one person in every community who is the "keeper of the history." Invite that person. Ministers know stories. Retired judges, principals and teachers know stories. The retired editor of the newspaper will be a valuable source of information. In the letter, ask them to watch for the upcoming newspaper article on *The Hero Next Door*. Give them the date and time for the community story conference and invite them to that conference. Allow time for the letter to arrive, then follow up with a phone call, stressing the importance of community involvement. There is no guarantee how many people will respond from the newspaper article, but you do want this core group to be at the community hero-search session.

When the day of the community story conference arrives, have everyone gather in one room. Have one of your students open the story session by explaining the mission of *The Hero Next Door*, then open the room to ideas. Let people tell the stories of those, from the past or present, who made a difference. Let one idea spark another idea. These sparks of creative electricity may produce a "hero next door" no one had even thought of before. As with any creative session, anything goes. There are no bad ideas. But, as the ideas arise, ask yourself if this story will "tell" in a short documentary. Remember, it's hard to tell a life story. It works better if you tell the story around a specific event.

Sometimes students will go along with what the adults think, just because they're, well, adults. Don't let that happen. This movie should be "owned" by the students. If you see students giving in to the adults' idea, allow the students the opportunity, later, when they're alone, to choose the hero-story that they really want to do.

At this point, you've done all you can do. You've involved the students and their families. Through the newspaper, you've invited and involved the community. Finally, sifting through it all, you've let the students pick their own hero-story. You're ready to begin your research.

RESEARCH

To research the hero you've decided upon, you will want to interview everyone who knows, or knew the person. It's great to interview the hero, but you don't have to. Interviewing people who know the hero will tell you a lot.

Go to your local library. Do old newspaper articles or photographs exist, telling about what this person did? Try to find significant landmarks in the person's life—the house where he grew up, the place where a significant event occurred. Through the mists of the research, the story will begin to form.

WRITING THE DOCUMENTARY

You don't have to write a script to produce a documentary, but you do need an outline to follow. You need to know who you're going to interview, the kinds of questions you're going to ask and where those questions are likely to take the story. (The questions should be ordered in such a way that the answers will tell the story.)

In making your outline, consider the same story beats we studied in the chapter on writing the screenplay:

1) Who was this person?

2) Where did this story take place? (the times, the mood, the political climate, etc.)

3) What was the problem?

4) What did the person do to attempt to solve that problem?

5.) What obstacles did this person encounter while making the effort to solve the problem?

These are the basics of human drama. It doesn't matter if it's a documentary—it's still a story. Conflict is the heart of every story. People want to be told the story of a human being struggling against powerful forces toward a worthy goal. A documentary movie, based on a true-life story, is an excellent way to reveal that human drama.

PREPARING FOR THE INTERVIEW

Interviewing a person on camera is not easy. Like all things, it gets easier with practice. If, in the beginning, your students feel like an octopus trying to waltz, they're right where most people are when they first try to do an on-camera interview.

Knowing that an on-camera interview can be challenging for the newcomer, we're going to approach these interviews using a method that makes them easier. Using this method, the student is free to make mistakes without worrying—because those mistakes will never show up in the movie.

Most professional on-camera interviews, like Bill Moyers on PBS, have two cameras going at once. One is on the person being interviewed. The other is on Bill Moyers. This is the best of all methods, because it gives you genuine responses from the interviewer and the person being interviewed.

But, it presents problems. You need two cameras, two microphones, two sets of lights. Technically, it's harder to light. Plus, the person doing the interview has to be skilled, experienced and confident because every question he asks will be on camera. There's no room for fumbling.

I know that your students are absolutely terrific, but let's give them an easier way to wade into this business of interviewing. It's also a way that will allow you to use one camcorder, one microphone and one set of lights.

PRACTICE THE INTERVIEW WITH OTHER STUDENTS

Before talking about production techniques, though, let's talk briefly about preparing for the interview. Not all of your students will be involved in asking the actual questions. Some students will be better on-camera than others. The students who want to be involved in asking the actual questions need to practice the interview.

First, they need to start with a list of questions. But they need to learn that they do not have to stick to those questions. Let's say the student interviewer asks a question about how the "hero" got the idea to do what he or she did. And, let's say that led to an answer that your earlier research did not reveal. The student does not have to simply go on to the next question on the list. If the person being interviewed says something that offers interesting information, the student-interviewer should feel free to explore that area. He needs to start with a list of pre-planned questions, but he is not required to stick to that list of questions. If the person being interviewed says something interesting, the student can explore that area, showing genuine interest and asking honest questions. If the student stammers and stumbles, trying to form questions, that's okay, because the stumbling won't be on camera, as you'll see in a minute.

PRODUCTION TECHNIQUES

Before you begin the interview, obviously, you know who you're going to interview. You've researched the subject and made a list of pre-planned questions. The students have practiced these questions on each other, but not on the person who is going to be interviewed. We want the interview to be fresh and spontaneous. If you practice with this person ahead of time, there is no way their answers can be spontaneous. The best thing movies can bring to the screen is emotion. Spontaneous answers are required to provide us with that much-needed emotion.

Once you know who you are interviewing, pick a location with a background that will be pertinent to this person's story. Pick a location where you can control the light and the sound. Remember, you cannot do an interview while battling street noise or the high school band practicing outside a nearby window. Consider all the things we talked about earlier in the book when choosing a location.

Once you have the subject and you've picked the background, it's time to set the camera, then the lights.

Put a student in the location where you want the person being interviewed to sit. (Pick a student who is approximately the same height and skin tone as the person you're about to interview. This student will be your "stand-in" for lighting purposes.) You don't want the person you're interviewing to be there yet. He or she should be scheduled to arrive in, say, an hour. The last thing you want is the person you're about to interview sitting around growing impatient because you're not ready.

Seat the student who is "standing in" for the interviewee and grab the camcorder. Plug the camcorder into a monitor or television. Have your camera person walk the camera around, composing different shots. Let the students pick the composition they like. If they compose a shot that does not work, ask them to consider why they chose that composition. Keep asking questions until they compose a shot that works. (For more about composition, refer to the earlier chapters.) Once you have a shot that you like for the interview, set the tripod and place the camera.

Have the student who is going to ask the questions sit right next to the camera, so that when the person being interviewed looks directly at the person asking the questions, the interviewee will be looking just off-camera.

With the student "stand-in" in place and with the camera in position, it's time to set the lights.

LIGHTING FOR THE INTERVIEW

There is no need to repeat the lessons we've talked about earlier on lighting. I just want to remind you that you will need a key light, your main source of light. Set that light first. The key light will create shadows on the opposite side of the interviewee's face (the side opposite the key light). Add a "fill light," on that side, to "fill" those shadows. If you can, add a "rim light" to the shoulders to separate the subject from the background. Since it's important that the audience see the background, add a light to illuminate the background. Adjust these lights, move them, add silks, if necessary, as discussed in the earlier chapter on lighting. And remember, as always, do not use electricity unless there is qualified adult supervision.

LIGHTING WITHOUT LIGHTING

It's not necessary to have electric lights to shoot an interview. We always have the sun. We can't set the sun where we want it, but we can set the person being interviewed where the sun will work for us. On a recent *Hero Next Door* project, the students wanted to interview an eighty-year-old man in the building where he had gone to school as a child. That old building did not have electricity, so the students planned their production around the sun. The sunlight came through a bank of windows from 12:00 to 3:30 every day. The students planned their shooting schedule around that sunlight and made a great movie. The subject's face was bathed in soft light, the same light that illuminated the background.

CAMERA

The same camera techniques discussed earlier in the book apply to the documentary. As mentioned, background is important. You want the background to help define the person you're interviewing. Seeing the person's face up close is important too. The question becomes, "when do you see the person's face up close?" That's part of the art of making documentary movies. If the person being interviewed is in a medium shot and, suddenly, she starts talking about something emotional, you want your camera person to slowly zoom in on her face. But, you can't say, "Zoom in." If you do, the person being interviewed will snap out of this moment and you'll lose it. This kind of thing has to be practiced when preparing to shoot the movie. This is where the camera person will need to follow her own best instincts about when to move in close, to see the soul of this human being.

As mentioned, have the person asking the questions sit right next to the camera. Don't ask the person being interviewed to talk directly into the camera. How expressive could you be if you were talking to a non-responsive, unemotional camera lens? Watch Bill Moyers do an interview. Notice how the people he is interviewing are looking off-camera, either right to left, or left to right. They are looking at Mr. Moyers. He is seated beside the camera.

SCREEN DIRECTION AND EYE-LINE IN THE INTERVIEW

The rules of screen direction will remain the same from the earlier chapters in the book. It's important, though, that we do a refresher course here for the purpose of the interview. As you know, the person being interviewed will be looking just off-camera. That means he or she will be looking either right to left, or left to right. To determine that, look at the nose. Which direction is it pointing? If the person being interviewed is looking, say, right to left, when you turn the camera around to videotape the student asking the questions, his nose should be pointing left to right. When you edit them together, it will appear as though they're talking to each other.

To make this conversation believable, it is also important that the eye-lines match. (Eye-line is covered earlier in the book and video.) Use your own common sense, when lining up the shots, to see if the eye-lines will match. They don't have to be perfect. They just have to be close enough for the audience to believe these two people are really, actually talking to each other.

Because, using our one-camera production technique, they're not really, actually talking to each other.

Here's how it works:

USING ONE CAMERA TO SHOOT AN INTERVIEW

The person you plan to interview arrives. You and your students welcome that person and make her comfortable. The chair where that person will sit is already in place. In fact, you have put small "markers" of tape on the floor where the chair legs go, just in case the chair is moved by mistake and you need to get it back into that exact place.

Have the person sit in the chair. Turn on the lights and look at the monitor, at the image of the person about to be interviewed. How does she look? Do you need to adjust lights? If so, do it quickly and safely (in other words, don't drop a light on her head).

Once the lights are set, have the sound person clip a lavaliere microphone to the person's shirt. The wire that leads from the microphone back to the camera should be hidden inside the person's shirt, if possible. To check the sound, have the person being interviewed look directly at the person who is about to ask the questions and speak in her normal tone of voice. Monitor this sound-check through headphones plugged into the camcorder. Have her move around to check for "clothes noise," the sound of the interviewee's clothes brushing against the microphone. If you hear clothes noise, reposition the microphone to correct the problem.

If the composition looks right, the lighting is effective, the eye-line is right and the sound is coming through without a problem, then you're ready to go.

...IT'S TIME TO ASK THE FIRST QUESTION

The student sits next to the camera. At this point, there is no camera on the student. The only camcorder you have is trained on the person being interviewed. The student can start by asking questions that will be easy for the interviewee to answer, allowing the interviewee and the student a chance to lose their jitters. After a while, the subject will begin to relax and warm up to the process.

The student should just keep asking the questions. When he hits an area that is fertile for good answers, he should use his own common sense to explore that area. It doesn't matter if he thinks he's asking "stupid" questions. He's not on camera. The person being interviewed will say many things that won't amount to much and other things that will have enormous value. Those moments are the heart of the documentary. We might be planning a twelve-minute video. To get that twelve minutes, we might shoot two hours of answers.

If the student asking the questions gets stumped, it's okay to stop. Let the students talk over what needs to be asked. Also, students are free to raise questions during the interview, but don't let the person being interviewed answer unless he is looking directly at the person doing the interview, so screen direction will be maintained in editing.

Finally, when you've asked all you know how to ask, take a break. Let the students discuss the interview for a few minutes. Have they covered everything? Is there anything else they wanted to ask? More answers are easy to get now. If that's all, the interview is over for that person. Thank her, get a release so you have the legal right to use her in the movie, then help carry her things to her car.

The next thing to do is meet with the class. Watch the video of the person being interviewed. Look for those parts where the person says things that can be added together to tell the story. Once you have the statements that you need to tell your story, then you'll need the questions. At this point, create a list of questions that will fit with the answers. Once those questions are ready, it's time to shoot your student-interviewer asking the questions on camera. Videotape the student asking the questions in the same location you used for the person being interviewed. This way, the background and the ambient sound will match.

If the person being interviewed was looking right to left, compose your student asking the questions, looking left to right, or vice versa. Do your best to make sure eye-lines match. The rule is, if you cut from a shot of the student asking the questions to a shot of the person giving the answer, will it look like they're talking to each other? If so, it's time to get the lights right, set the microphone and prepare to shoot footage of the student, looking just off camera, asking the prepared questions.

You don't want the student staring off into space, asking questions to someone who is not there. Put the director in front of the student asking the questions. In fact, give her the questions (you don't want to see the person asking the questions holding a piece of paper) and let her feed the questions to the student-interviewer. If the director does not like the way the student delivered a question, she can ask him to do it again, coaching him on each take. There's no reason to turn off the camera between takes. Videotape is cheap. Keep rolling, doing take after take of the same question, until — finally — the actor-interviewer has asked all the questions that need to be asked. Once the questions are ready, and you've interviewed all the people you plan to interview, it's time to edit.

EDITING THE DOCUMENTARY

How do you edit a documentary? You make it interesting. Have the interviewer ask a question. Have the person being interviewed answer the question. Through questions and answers, build a story that makes the audience care. There is not one "right way" to do it. Follow your own instincts. Tell a story that makes you care.

In making documentaries, we call the on-camera interview the A-roll. We call all the other footage the B-roll. B-roll might be video footage of old photographs, or old motion picture footage from home movies. If the person being interviewed is talking about, say, a Civil Rights march in which she participated, B-roll could be photographs of that march. Your storytelling sense will guide you as to when it's right to stay on the person being interviewed and when it's right to cut to the B-roll.

RE-ENACT SCENES

Have you watched *Unsolved Mysteries* on television? If so, you've seen good examples of re-enacting scenes and editing those scenes with the person being interviewed.

Let's say a woman is being interviewed about discovering a stolen car, hidden in the woods. While she's talking, the *Unsolved Mysteries* editor might cut to re-enactment footage of an actress, portraying the woman, coming upon the same kind of car, out in the woods. The actress in the re-enacted scene will look different from the woman being interviewed, but the audience is willing to go along with that because they understand it's part of telling this kind of story.

In *The Hero Next Door* episode *The Woman Who Painted The Klan Sign Yellow*, Brodie Reed, now in her eighties, told the story of when she stood up to the Ku Klux Klan back in the 1950s. The Klan had done something horrible and cowardly in her town in 1958. The Klan also had a sign at the city limits that welcomed people to town. Brodie Reed didn't think that the Klan should be welcoming anybody to town, so she rode out to the edge of town and painted the Klan sign yellow—for coward.

The Klan came after her, but Brodie Reed stood her ground. The point I'm trying to make here, though, is how the students re-enacted scenes from Brodie Reed's interview and edited them into the movie.

There was a scene in which Brodie Reed talked about driving out to the sign and painting it yellow. The students called around town and found a 1956 Ford. One of the moms dressed up in 1950s dress, shoes and hairstyle. The students recreated the sign out of plywood, from descriptions provided by people who had seen it. The mom, portraying Brodie, drove out to the sign in the '56 Ford and painted the sign yellow.

Brodie Reed telling the story on-camera (the A-roll) was interesting, but it made it even more dramatic when the students re-enacted certain scenes.

Your own good story-telling instincts will tell you what to dramatize. If the person you're interviewing is talking about something dramatic, dramatize that. The only thing stopping you might be technical challenges. If you're interviewing someone about flying an airplane in the 1920s, you could hardly re-enact that scene unless you had access to a 1920s airplane. But you could cut to shots of old photographs, or even motion picture footage from that person's old home movies, or from the Library of Congress in Washington, D.C. (The Library of Congress and The National Archives are filled with wonderful historic footage and photographs. The cost is minimal. Some collections of these historic photographs are searchable on their websites at www.loc.gov and www.nara.gov).

Dramatizing, or re-enacting, certain scenes is all part of the fun of *The Hero Next Door*. Dramatizing scenes also gives your students the experience of acting, directing, casting, props, wardrobe, dramatic lighting, editing—and all the other lessons taught earlier in the book. The on-camera interview and re-enacting scenes give your students the opportunity to gain a wide range of production experience. And, remember, experience is the true teacher!

INSERT EDITING

There is a certain kind of editing you need to be able to do in order to re-enact scenes and edit them together with the person being interviewed. It's called insert editing. To explain insert editing, let's go back to the example of *Unsolved Mysteries*. The person is being interviewed on-camera. At a certain point, the editor cuts away to the dramatization of the scene that the person is talking about. We see the dramatization while we continue to hear the on-camera person talking about what happened. Adding the video footage of the re-enactment, without interrupting the audio of the on-camera interview, is called "insert editing."

Not every editing machine will do insert editing. Editing from a camcorder to a VCR cannot give you insert editing. If you're considering editing on a non-linear system, as described in "Digital Editing," be sure to make it clear to your salesperson that you must be able to do insert editing. Insert editing is simple, and it's a powerful movie-making technique, but you must make sure you get an editing machine that will do insert editing.

One way to achieve the same result as insert editing, when editing from a VCR to a VCR, is to add the audio as voice-over in the mix phase of post-production. Read the chapter on editing on the VCR. In the second stage of that process (VEM-2), there are lessons about how to re-record the on-camera person's voice to audiotape, then add that voice to your movie in the final mix.

The most important thing required for movie making is not an editing machine. It's desire. If you can only edit from camcorder to VCR, or VCR to VCR, that's fine. It gives you the chance to become a creative problem-solver.

STILL PHOTOGRAPHS

Still photographs work well in a documentary. If the person on camera is talking about the airplane he flew in the 1920s, cut to a still photograph of that same man, in his younger days, standing next to the airplane.

To get the old photos into your movie, you must, somehow, get the photograph onto videotape. One way to do that is to affix the old photo, temporarily, to a stiff piece of cardboard. Put the cardboard on an easel, or pin it to the wall. Light the photo from the side (not straight on) with soft light, so the light does not reflect off the photo. Set your camcorder up in front of the photograph and shoot video footage of the actual photo. You can pan across the photo. Tilt up or down. Zoom in or out. Do whatever your storytelling instincts tell you in order to add movement to the photos and help bring them to life.

WHAT REALLY MATTERS IN A DOCUMENTARY?

The human heart. That's what always matters in a movie. The way to get that is to see the human telling the story. See her eyes. Hear her soul. Feel what she feels. The technical aspects of a documentary do not matter as much as the heart. The audience is forgiving if a microphone happens to dip into a shot, or if the camera is shaky or if the lighting is not perfect. None of that matters much if you get the human soul into your movie. That's always what matters.

DISTRIBUTION AND THE FUTURE

The Hero Next Door will be promoted in every school in the country. Schools, service organizations and local government will work together, in a synergistic effort, to find their heroes and tell their stories.

We're betting that communities will be proud of their heroes and will want to share them with the world through:

1) The Make A Movie.Net trading post. Any organization can post information about their *Hero Next Door* project and trade their movies through the U.S. mail.

2) The next step will be a "screening room" on the Make A Movie.Net website. The best of *The Hero Next Door* projects will be streamed, over the internet, from our web site to any school in the world.

3) Our vision is to include the best *Hero Next Door* stories in our own reality-based television program, complete with an on-camera star-host. The show will be produced in the style of *Unsolved Mysteries*. The students will do an "A" camera interview with the hero, while re-enacting certain scenes. A segment might be three minutes or ten minutes, depending upon how long it takes to tell the heart of the story. The star-host will hold the segments together through on-camera and voice-over narration. The school, or other organization, that produces the segment will be paid for the use of their *Hero Next Door* episode, if chosen.

This will be the only show on television with stories discovered, written, produced and directed by students. Students will watch because it's "their show." The adult audience will watch because each story will carry a message that people want to hear over and over again—that human beings on this earth can make a difference if they have the courage to do the right thing.

Many young people today feel that their lives don't matter. *The Hero Next Door* gives them the opportunity to make a movie, and—at the same time—learn that anybody on earth can make a difference if they choose to do so.

These are the stories of the people who hold the world together. They deserve to be told. Discover the stories in your town and share them with the world.

*   *   *

Hero Next Door

Production Check List

Creating a *Hero Next Door* episode is a step-by-step process. Let's take a look at what you need.

1) You need desire — a core group of students who want to make a movie. They don't have to know how. That's what this training program is about. They just have to "want to." They may be scared and unsure. That's normal when any human approaches the unknown. But they have to have, somewhere inside, the desire to make a movie. It doesn't have to be all of the students, just some of the students.

   You need a principal who has desire. It has been my experience that principals love projects that bring the school together with the community. *The Hero Next Door* does that in an excellent way. Students learn to make movies while also learning the history that is right under their noses. In *the Hero Next Door* episode *You Can't Change If You Can't Vote*, Mr. Ezra Cunningham was talking about taking sandwiches to the people marching from Selma to Montgomery during the Civil Rights movement. One of the students making the movie asked Mr. Cunningham where they got the sandwiches. He answered, "Your grandmother made them." I will always remember the light that went on in that girl's eyes when she learned her grandmother had played a part in local history. I think she saw, then, that she, too, could be part of local history.

   If your principal has concerns about where this will fit into the curriculum, it has been my experience that it fits perfectly into history, social studies or, of course, any kind of journalism or communications class. Do you have a Social Studies Fair in your school district? If you do a *Hero Next Door* project, I'll bet you a nickel that you win.

2) You need a "hero next door." As one teacher put it, "There's enormous value in making the movie, but at least half the value is in the process of finding the 'hero'." I believe that's true. These heroes are everywhere. You just have to look for them. And it's always fun to find a hero where you didn't know one existed. This search can involve the local newspaper, local churches, citizen groups like the Sierra Club and service organizations like, say, the Kiwanis Club. Make *The Hero Next Door* project a joint venture between the school and a local organization and you'll get all kinds of support.

3) You may need money. If so, get a local sponsor. Remember, your movie is something that can easily be duplicated and seen by hundreds, maybe thousands, of people in your area. Does your local cable company have a public access channel? Many companies would be proud to sponsor a *Hero Next Door* project. It would be good advertising for them and might also be a tax write-off.

4) You need a camcorder. One of our mottoes in this program is "Anyone who can borrow a camcorder from Aunt Ethel and a VCR from Uncle Fred can make a movie." That's true. Any camcorder will do. But the better the camcorder, the better the picture and audio.

The best consumer (not professional) camcorder is a digital camcorder with three chips. This gives you the best picture and audio, while also allowing you the ability to edit digitally without losing picture quality. These camcorders are very inexpensive for what they will do. Your school may not own one, but someone in your community may have one they'd be willing to loan your class for this "community cause." If the owner is nervous about the camcorder being broken, let him be present for the interview. Some churches have audio-visual programs, which may include a digital camcorder. Your local camera store may loan you a digital camcorder as long as you put their name on your movie as being one of the sponsors. Make the movie in any way that you can, but a digital camcorder will give you the best results. If your *Hero Next Door* episode is going to be on our television program, it is best if it is shot on a digital camcorder. If you cannot get a digital camcorder contact us at heronextdoor@makeamovie.net. We may be able to loan you a digital camcorder for the length of your project.

5) You'll need a microphone. A lavaliere microphone that plugs into the camcorder works great for the on-camera interview. If you can't get a lavaliere microphone, though, go back and read the chapter on recording sound. Follow those guidelines, and you'll be fine. Only as a last resort should you use the microphone that is attached to the camcorder. You will not be happy with that result.

6) You need research. In doing the research you will form a list of questions that, with answers, will add up to tell the story of your hero next door and what he or she did that has made a difference to the community.

7) You need to pick the student or students who will ask the questions. Once chosen, those students need to practice interviewing. Part of that practice is learning to leave the list of questions and pursue a line of questioning that may have value.

One technique the student needs to understand about interviewing on camera is to not make any kind of sound. When people listen in a normal conversation, they often voice their approval with sounds like, "Okay, Um hmmm, Uh huh or Wow." When doing an on-camera interview, however, the interviewer's voice will pick up on the sound track of the person being interviewed. This will cause problems later in editing. The student-interviewer needs to understand that, when listening to an answer, he is free to nod his approval but not to mumble, "Uh huh, Um hmmm, Okay, or Wow."

8) You'll need a location to interview the people on-camera. These interviews can be with the hero, or with people who know, or knew, the hero.

9) After the on-camera people have been interviewed, you'll need to turn the camera around and videotape the student interviewer asking the questions.

10) When videotaping the student asking questions, you will need to shoot the student "reacting" to the person being interviewed. This is a very important point, so do not forget it. The person on-camera will be talking and, from time to time, you will want to cut to the student-interviewer listening, or reacting. Videotape the student asking the questions, then, at the end of the session, shoot, say, three minutes of student reacting in different ways, listening intently or smiling at a humorous statement. You won't use all of the three minutes, but three minutes should give you enough of the various reactions you will need. Review the chapters in the book that talk about the "cutaway" shot.

11) You will need to consider shooting a master shot that includes all of the students involved in the production. When you need to cut away from the person being interviewed on camera, you could cut to the interviewer reacting, or you could cut to a master shot of the entire crew. One student will be in the act of shooting camera. Another student might be holding a light, or the boom pole for the microphone. The master works well as a cutaway shot. It's also a good shot to include all of the students in the movie. Just make sure you maintain screen direction as described earlier in the book. (Note: If you shoot a master of the crew, you will need to provide a "prop camera" for the crew, because you will be shooting with your "real" camera. If, for example, you're shooting your movie with a digital camcorder, let the crew in this staged master use any camcorder, even one that doesn't work. It will only be serving as a prop.

12) You need to re-enact certain scenes, as is done in shows like *Unsolved Mysteries* and *911*. Re-enacting two or three scenes should be enough. All of the lessons for re-enacting scenes can be found earlier in this book.

13) You need a way to edit your video. That can be done tape to tape, or it can be done digitally, as described in the chapter "Digital Editing." To edit the movie properly, you'll need an editing machine capable of insert editing, as described earlier in this chapter.

14) If you want people outside your community to see your *Hero Next Door* episode, you'll need a way to distribute it. Make A Movie.Net offers a distribution channel, on our website at www.makeamovie.net.

TECHNO-FRIGHT AND TECHNICAL SUPPORT

Some teachers are afraid of the technical side of movie making. I understand. I'm afraid of those technical gadgets too. Knowledge drives away fear. It has been my experience that if you sit down and practice with the camcorder or the editing machine, it's not that hard. Plus, you'll be proud of yourself when you actually learn it.

If you're still too scared to get started, though, there is a way to get support. We have a database which will help us find qualified videographers who live in, or near, your community. These people may do weddings or corporate videos. Either way, he or she will own quality video equipment and will be experienced with camera, lighting, sound and editing.

This person may not know one thing about doing an on-camera interview. That's fine. You and your students can handle that part. This technical consultant will be there for one reason — to hold your hand through the technical side of movie making. Let me define "hand holding." This movie should be produced by your students. Based upon the lessons they've learned in this book and video training program, they should compose the shots. They should set the lights. They should place the microphone. The technical consultant is there to help. When they make a mistake, it is the consultant's job to guide them back to what will work. The goal is, by the end of the day, to have video and audio that work well. But the students should do it. The technical consultant is there to provide equipment and guide you and the students through the technical challenges.

There are three ways to compensate this technical consultant:

1) He or she might do it for no charge, looking upon this as community service, or as a way to advertise. If the consultant does wedding videos, she might see your students and their families as potential sources of income for future wedding videos.

2) If the consultant is a professional, with expensive equipment, he or she may want to be paid. I understand that. I like to be paid, and so do you. In that case, you may be able to pay them with money from your school's budget or with money from your movie's sponsor.

3) A third option is that you pay part of it, and we'll pay part of it. Make A Movie.Net is looking for grant money to subsidize *Hero Next Door* productions.

Do not use this technical consultant as a crutch. If you can make your *Hero Next Door* episode on your own, do it. But if you're not going to start your movie because you're afraid of the technical side of things, then contact us. We are here to help you win, no matter what!

So, there you have it! With that kind of technical support, there is no reason to not get started. You have no excuse left. You have to do it.

I started this chapter by quoting Margaret Mead.

"Never doubt that a small group of thoughtful, committed people can change the world. Indeed it is the only thing that ever has."

I'd like to close by reminding you that you are one of those people.

Hero Next Door stories are in every community in the world. They're in your community. Find your stories. Let's share them with the world.

NOTES:

Support, Distribution, & the Future

By now, you know 90% of the rules of filmmaking that Spielberg knows. I didn't say you know 90% of what Spielberg knows. His experience has taught him vast amounts more than you know. But you know 90% of the basic rules of movie making, plenty enough to get started. Getting started is the most important thing you can do right now. If you wait until you know more, so you can be perfect, you'll never start. It's time to get into action. Getting into action leads you to experience, and experience is the best teacher.

If you're afraid your movies will be bad, that's normal. Just remember the lesson from the chapter on "Story & Screenplay"— there are no bad ideas, because all bad ideas lead to good ideas. The same is true for movies — all bad movies lead to good movies.

I have a friend who wrote ten screenplays before she sold one. She would finish a screenplay, mail it off, then hurry home and start the next one. It was a good system. If the studio didn't like her first script, it didn't bother her because she was already halfway through the next one which she liked even better. Finally, she sold one. Since then, she's made zillions of dollars writing movies. Her slogan was and is: "The only way to fail is to quit." So don't worry about failing. The only way you can fail is to quit. The only person who can quit is you. So, just don't quit.

SUPPORT

Some people quit when they get stuck, bogged down in a problem, like—for example—the technical side of editing. That's why I built several levels of support into this program—so there is no way you can get stuck and quit.

1) The video. It's designed to clarify some of the lessons in the book.

2) The web site. If you're still stuck, e-mail your question to support@makeamovie.net. We'll do our best to answer your question on our bulletin board so you can benefit from the answer—and so the other members of our nationwide youth group production team can also benefit.

3) Telephone support. For an added fee, you may call the phone number found on the back of the title page of this book for telephone support. I will coach you through any problem, from story to camera to editing on video. Would you like your class to have a story conference? Gather your students around a speaker phone, and we'll have a story conference—just like in Hollywood.

4) Seminars. Make A Movie.Net offers seminars, during the week and on weekends. We'll come to your school, church, synagogue or youth center. Call us or check the Make A Movie.Net web site for more information.

TEACHING RESOURCES

Teaching and production resources will be available on our web site. We'll put a couple of short screenplays on the web site. Use them to learn, or to produce. If your group writes a script you're proud of, we might put it on the web site for others to use. It's fun to see how two different groups might treat the same screenplay.

There will be forms for items like production strips, storyboards and pencil edits. We will also make sample releases available, like a property release, or a release for actors. These are sample releases only. Make A Movie.Net does not offer legal advice. Plus, requirements for a legal release may vary from state to state.

DISTRIBUTION

The first movies you make may be just for fun. You won't want anybody to see them but your group. You'll laugh at the mistakes—and you'll learn. After a while, though, you're going to make a movie that you'll want to share. One way to do that is through the Make A Movie.Net Trading Post. E-mail the title of your video, along with a few words describing your story, to our web site. If another school is interested in seeing your movie, a teacher from that school will contact you directly, and you will mail them your video.

When e-mailing information to us about your movie, be sure to include the name of your organization, your street address and your telephone number. We encourage you to only trade videos with an organization that has a verifiable name, address and telephone number. You don't know who you're dealing with on the internet. If you're mailing your video to a church, synagogue, school, YMCA or other organization with a verifiable phone number and address, you should be okay.

MAKE A MOVIE.NET: VIDEO STREAMING

Video streaming is the next big thing on the internet. Video streaming simply means you'll be able to watch real movies, in real-time, over the internet. No distributors. No mailing videotapes back and forth. Just come to our web site screening room, find a student-produced movie you want to see, click on it and watch it. It will be a great way for your students to share their movies and meet other movie-making kindred spirits.

Steven Spielberg has forecast that the internet will eventually become the primary source for entertainment. Appearing on NBC's *Today Show*, Spielberg told co-host Katie Couric: "I think that the internet is going to affect the most profound change on the entertainment industries combined. And we're all gonna be tuning in to the most popular internet show in the world, which will be coming from some place in Des Moines."

That show could be produced by your students.

CAMP HOLLYWOOD

One of the dreams we have for the future is "Camp Hollywood." Every summer we'll shoot a feature film at one of the summer camps—a professional eight-week production, designed to be sold to the public. Students from across the country who have shown real interest in our program will have the opportunity to attend the camp and work on the movie for two weeks, alongside professionals. When they leave Camp Hollywood, their production ability will have shot light years ahead. When the movie comes to their home town, they can brag about what they did on their summer vacation. Camp Hollywood depends upon your level of interest. If you're interested, let us know by e-mail or at our post office address on the back of the title page of this book.

FUND RAISING FOR MOVIE FINANCING

The promise of this program is to teach you how to make a movie, using equipment you already own. But, there are instances where you may need to raise money. Let's look at some fun ways to raise "production capital."

1) Once your students have gained some ability with the equipment, they could video weddings, complete with editing, music and voice-over narration. How about a "build-up" story for how the couple met?

2) Church video albums and school video yearbooks are popular and can be profitable.

3) Parents are busy at their children's birthday parties, with guests, party favors and presents. Many parents might pay your students to video the party.

4) Some home owners pay for articles from their home to be photographed onto a video inventory, for insurance purposes. In the event of fire or theft, the video inventory could help with the claim. Your local insurance agent might be glad to direct your students to some of his clients.

5) T-shirts are a great item for fund raising. We'll have a few of our own designs that you can sell as fundraisers.

6) Sell Make A Movie.Net popcorn to raise money for your productions. Popcorn is synonymous with movies, so it can provide your students with the perfect pitch to explain their project.

E-mail your fund raising ideas, and we'll put them on the website for all to benefit.

GET INTO ACTION!

Young people today spend an enormous amount of time watching television. The stories they experience, for the most part, come in the form of movies. The Make A Movie.Net educational program will empower some of those young people to learn to tell stories in the way they know best. Some of them will get very good at it.

These are empowering times. To think that a student can pick up a camcorder, make a movie and broadcast that movie to the world—all for a very small amount of money—is, to me, nothing short of a miracle.

There's an old poem that says, "Hitch your wagon to a star." A "star" is passing now. Give your students their chance to grab that star and tell their stories to the world.

In the book mentioned earlier, *Rebel Without a Crew*, a studio executive complimented Robert Rodriguez on what she referred to as his "first film." That night, in his diary, Rodriguez wrote, "She complimented me on my 'first film.' This was my first feature film," he added in his diary, "but she didn't know about my other twelve."

Now it's your turn.

Write a story, pick up a camcorder and go make your "first twelve."